HELD

Tyndale House Publishers, Inc.
Carol Stream, Illinois

to be
comforted

to be
loved

to be...

HELD

Leslie Haskin
9-11 SURVIVOR

Visit Tyndale's exciting Web site at www.tyndale.com

Check out the latest about Leslie Haskin at www.safehugs.com

Library of Congress Cataloging-in-Publication Data

Haskin, Leslie D.
    Held / Leslie Haskin.
        p. cm.
    Includes bibliographical references.
    ISBN-13: 978-1-4143-1222-4 (sc)
    ISBN-10: 1-4143-1222-9 (sc)
    1. Suffering—Religious aspects--Christianity. I. Title.
    BV4905.3.H384 2007
    248.8'6--dc22   2007014881

Printed in the United States of America

13 12 11 10 09 08 07
 7   6   5   4   3   2   1

CONTENTS

ACKNOWLEDGMENTS

First, there is God my Father.

Over the past few years I have been through the fire. There have been dark nights and difficult questions—sometimes more questions than answers. But in the face of doubt, I've gained greater insight from being in the presence of God. He is everything to me.

This book was made possible because His wisdom placed me in the pews of a church with a mission of healing and in the care of my pastor, John Torres, and his wife, Shannon, who teach God's love and lead by example. Thank you.

Thank you also to my brother and friend, Pastor Lawrence Haskin, whose many words of wisdom, teachings, and encouragement can be found throughout these pages. You are incredible.

In the face of my many questions, fears, and a healing journey that sometimes seemed impossible, all of you were there. Therefore, I dedicate this book to your work and your mission fields: Goodwill Church in Montgomery, New York, and Household of Faith Church in Markham, Illinois.

Continue in God's grace . . .

INTRODUCTION

Father,
It is again with great expectation that I come to You this night.
I ask only that Your healing words flood these pages and that
Your unparalleled greatness brings peace. Pour out Your Holy
Spirit, Father, for deliverance in the lives of those who suffer
still from tragedy, disappointment, and heartbreak. Restore
hope in situations we might interpret as hopeless. Lift our
visions higher than our circumstances, so that Your glory is
revealed; let Your will be done. Bring healing, Father, and
bring peace. I ask for the sake of the Kingdom of Heaven
alone. Amen.

Hurricane Katrina was one of our nation's worst natural disasters. The loss of life and destruction still seem immeasurable. My heartfelt sympathy goes out to the countless survivors who lost their loved ones, their homes, their possessions, their mementos, and all that was familiar to them.

I also remain faithful in my prayers for the victims of Hurricane Rita, the Rwandan genocide, and the terrorist attacks of September 11, 2001.

It is these events and others that motivated me to pen words of encouragement once more.

I believe that God is amazing in what He will use to touch

our hearts and free us, and I'm honored that He allowed me to step forward in that regard.

Even today, I find myself acknowledging His dominion all over again. When I consider my life and all that I have survived, the veil is lifted. For what I once thought to be the end of my story actually became the beginning.

Who would have thought that after a successful climb up the corporate ladder to a six-figure income, a beautiful home, and all the benefits that "my world" afforded me, terror would strike? Who could have foreseen my great fall and subsequent landing amid the muck and the mire of mental illness, homelessness, Post-Traumatic Stress Disorder, and inability to explain my sudden exile from the world?

Nevertheless, these pages go beyond just me.

Held is everybody's story.

It is an exhaustive look at the daily struggles of survivors whose lives have been crushed by the weight of murder, cancer, AIDS, terror, and natural disaster. Those left hyperventilating and wondering about the mercies of God.

It is a deep dive into the uncertainties of spirituality and fear, in order to retrieve a message of hope—that all who enter here might come to know the essential Jesus Christ—so for the next few hours, days, or even weeks of your attention you might understand what is the hope of His calling. My contributions to the Kingdom then move beyond simply remembering each September after September, into the realm of imparting hope beyond what seems hopeless and declaring the good news to those who might not have otherwise believed.

The good news: No matter the life-shattering circumstance that delivers the devastating blow to our spirit,
God is bigger. He is faithful and unchanging, merciful and
consistent with His offer to us, that through it all, we will
be comforted, we will be loved, we will be *Held*. You are
confronted again and again with the choice of letting God
speak or letting your wounded self cry out. Although
there has to be a place where you can allow your wounded
part to get the attention it needs, your vocation is to speak
from the place in you where God dwells.

—HENRI J. M. NOUWEN

CHAPTER 1

ONCE UPON A TIME

When Towers Fall

I woke up one late-summer morning, and the rain was falling. The
thunder rolled gently at times, and the air was thick with humidity.
Somewhere off in the distance, every now and then, a quick flash of
light came near and startled me. Normally, on a day like this one,
I'd stay in bed with the rain and drift in and out of sleep patterns
brought on by the melodic arrangement of raindrops falling on
my windows. However, this day was different. It was annoying. It
interfered with my plans.

It was Friday morning. It had been a long, stressful week, and

I was looking forward to a day of relaxing. I had started on Sunday cleaning my new home in preparation for the move-in, which took three full days. Moving my belongings into the house from the storage unit that I'd rented earlier that summer took two more days, and I hadn't even started unpacking boxes. I was exhausted.

My plan was to take a full day, sit alone in front of the nearby water's edge, and take inventory of where God had brought me. I'd enjoy a picnic and a time of prayerful meditation reflecting back on the long summer I'd spent being homeless, enduring a long list of calamities, suffering due losses, and surviving frequent panic attacks.

I'd sit by the water. I'd tell God of my complete surrender to His will, and then He'd renew my strength. It was the perfect plan. Prescription to my mind. It would take place at the only place a peaceful revival could happen—at the water's edge.

Hours passed, the rain kept falling, and my frustration grew. I stood at my front door watching the drowning grass until suddenly, I recalled God's promise. Specifically, His Word declares that by faith we could move mountains. *Wow, what if . . . ?* I thought.

My mind raced through the Word of God, collecting all that I could remember about faith. Every Scripture served to feed the flame of anticipation as I considered the implication of that promise. "Supped up" in minutes by the possibilities, I braced myself to move the rain. I collected all the authority that my voice could muster and started telling the rain to stop—"In Jesus' name, stop raining," I shouted, with authority. I could even feel myself getting all emotional about it. Tears came to my eyes, my fists got tighter as I pounded them in the air, and you know what—it kept raining. In fact, I think that's about the time that the once-subtle rain was officially upgraded to a tropical storm. It fell in torrents.

Finally and sadly, after a few more loud commands to the unresponsive downpour, I gave up. I took my picnic blanket out of the basket that I'd placed it in, spread it across the floor in my then-empty house, and sat near the window and cried.

I was convinced that God was once again getting it wrong. "How could You, God? How could You ignore my needs in this way? You said that You would supply all of my needs according to all that You have. Yet, here I am, completely spent, and You deny me rest. What does this mean? What have I done wrong to You?"

My spirit, just in sheer gloom, collapsed to the floor. I don't know exactly how long I kvetched before the Lord before I fell asleep to the sound of the falling rain. Newly formed and gentle breezes met me there underneath the window, and I do believe I snored.

I woke a few hours later to the dripping of the final raindrops and the smell of rain in the air. The sun was going down, and the sky was a magnificent orange. Crickets were chirping, and moisture had settled on the ledge. I reveled in it. Looking around at the beauty and richness of what the rain had produced, I quickly realized what God had done. I understood what *faith* really means. Faith is letting God do His thing despite our own desires. It's allowing Him to give us those things that we have need of . . . in the way that He knows to be best. Faith is about trusting beyond what our eyes can see and what our situations dictate.

> Faith: It's letting God do His thing despite our own desires.

I asked the Lord to stop the rain so that I could pack a bag, drive to a nearby lake, and have a picnic that I thought would give me some much-needed time of quiet and rest. He brought the rain down harder so that I could just stop—be still even—sit quietly near the window, be lulled by the soothing sound of the rain, and be "quieted" to rest.

Life is like that sometimes, I think. We will often find ourselves in situations that we cannot plan our way out of and in places that we never planned to be in to begin with. We find that even with all of our best-laid plans and careful attention to detail, life is still beyond our control.

I learned a small bit of that lesson six years ago. And, as I reflect back, comparing what I know now, I must admit, I am still learning. Even so, I remember it like it was yesterday—September 11, 2001.

I woke that morning as I did every other weekday, dressed in my designer finest and all my arrogance, and was off to my executive position atop Tower One of the World Trade Center.

I remember that the day was particularly beautiful. The birds were singing, and the air was filled with the fragrance of freshly cut grass. The sky was a brilliant blue, and the sun cast a magnificent yellow glow over the earth. The mountains near my home seemed to capture sunlight and cast iridescent shadows over my backyard.

I wanted to play hooky from work that day and relax in the beauty of the mountains where I lived. Instead, I took the two-hour train ride into New York City, as I did every morning, to my office on the thirty-sixth and thirty-seventh floors of Tower One.

I arrived in the usual eight o'clock hour, which, according to building standards, was a little late. Most people were already in their offices and working by that time. After reading a few e-mails and having my usual cranberry muffin and hazelnut coffee, I walked over to my assistant's desk to get some answers to a problem that, the night before, had escalated to my level.

My assistant's desk was directly in front of the window.

As I stood talking with her, midsentence and without warning, thunder literally crashed into the building. I heard it and felt it simultaneously. It came from around us, beneath us, and on top of us at the same time. Items rolled off the desks, lights flickered, and windows exploded. Loud bangs resonated from all over the office while people were running and screaming and looking for a passable way out. In only seconds, the ceiling above us was beginning to buckle, and fire was escaping through once obscure seams in the ceiling.

I just stood there in front of that window, frozen in time as my universe collapsed around me. I stood there staring at what five minutes before was a gorgeous view of the city—now forever darkened by falling body parts, furniture, paper, and debris banging against the sides of the building. I felt a warm stream of water run down the inside of my leg.

I stood there for a few minutes desperately trying to collect what remained of my mind and really understand what was happening. Instead, being completely absent from my body, I followed the crowd down thirty-six floors of smoke and blood and body parts and explosions and a fire so angry and intense that it charred even the concrete that was once our playground.

By the time I reached the concourse level where we escaped the building, I was literally stepping over decapitated human remains and witnessing torn pieces of flesh splattered across the remaining glass where my friends and colleagues jumped or fell or were pushed from the upper floors. I can still see them falling.

What was left of my mind was lost in those moments. What was once my lost soul was recovered by God.

In the months that followed, I suffered a mental breakdown and was diagnosed with severe Post-Traumatic Stress Disorder. When I recalled the events of that day, I spoke with a severe stutter. I boarded my windows with thick shutters and was afraid that the Taliban were living in the shed in my backyard. I stayed awake for days at a time holding on to weapons that I'd placed near my bed. I couldn't go in my basement for fear that the ceiling would collapse on top of me, and going anywhere other than a corner store was impossible. My prognosis was not good. The doctors thought that I would never return to a productive state of mind.

Then one night, when there was nothing bigger than my fears and anxiety, God sent a tiny miracle to my bedside and restored my soul. I'll tell you more about that later.

It's interesting for me now, looking back at what I was before

September 11 and seeing what God has birthed in me since that day. My life, even from my own eyes, is an amazing witness of God's grace and healing powers.

As I began my journey of healing, I began to know God, and I let Him know me. For the first time in my life, I honestly shared my whole self with my Father, and it changed me from the inside.

Under the light of His eyes, I have learned the truth about life. It is, in its true nature, endlessly compassionate, beautiful, peaceful, and full of joy and love. It is also chaos and confusion, sickness, death, pain, and tragedy. It is what I now know to be an all-encompassing journey, no part of which is in our control.

Knowing what I know, I have to believe that God sees our darkest nights and knows exactly how to bring light to every situation. Our quiet rain and individual storms do not shake Him, and falling towers don't catch Him by surprise. He is God, and our lives and all the details of our lives, big and small, are but the unfolding of His eternal purpose, even when it rains. Our lives are all part of one huge, comprehensive plan to return us to the original place of intent.

I am now on a mission to live that plan more completely. To embrace it and live an authentic life, knowing God more intimately than ever before. To speak His truth and not my own. And as I come to know Him more, I am empowered to live the "all encompassing" parts of life and His great plan in complete surrender to them.

> I am now on a mission to live an authentic life, knowing God more intimately than ever before.

I am learning, relearning, and then learning again how to place all of who I am—the good and the bad—at the foot of the cross and leave it there. I'm learning and relearning to speak my requests to God and then listen to what it is that I need.

Over the past several months, I have met many people on this road to enlightenment, this road to Damascus. I have heard many stories of healing, revelation, and personal encounters with Christ. Though the stories vary at some point, each began on a normal day doing normal things. Each of us experienced the trauma to our core, on levels that we didn't even know existed within our hearts, and then we saw the light. Each of us found it difficult, if not impossible, to surrender each layer, one layer at a time, probing through the whys and the hows, before we were transformed.

How sweet is the journey when accompanied by Him? How bearable is the road when He leads?

Yet, even as I walk steadfastly in life near Him, life keeps happening. I am amazed at the situations I find myself in after planning and sweating for a specific result, or after "telling" God how to give to me or what He should do in order to provide for my needs. I'm even more amazed to discover, now that He's redeemed me, what my needs really were. So much so that I am investing and trusting in God's grace, which is the flavor of future expectation.

Follow me as I follow Christ.

CHAPTER 2

SLEEPER CELLS, TSUNAMIS, AND EARTHQUAKES, OH MY!

What's Bigger than This?

At 3:42 a.m. on July 28, 1976, while unsuspecting citizens slept, Tangshan, a city in northeastern China, was hit by a magnitude 7.8 earthquake. The earthquake struck an area where it was totally unexpected and obliterated the entire city, killing over 240,000 people—making it the deadliest earthquake of the twentieth century.

On September 11, 2001, nineteen al-Qaeda terrorists hijacked four commercial passenger jets and crashed two of them, United

Airlines Flight 175 and American Airlines Flight 11, into the World Trade Center in New York City. A third airplane, American Airlines Flight 77, was crashed into the Pentagon in Arlington County, Virginia. Passengers and members of the flight crew on the fourth plane, United Airlines Flight 93, crashed into a field near Shanksville, Pennsylvania. In addition to the 19 hijackers, 2,973 people died.

On May 2, 2004, Gazan Arabs murdered a Jewish mother in her eighth month of pregnancy and her four children, spraying their car with bullets and then shooting each child repeatedly at point-blank range.

On August 23, 2005, a tropical storm formed over the Bahamas and crossed southern Florida as a moderate Category 1 hurricane. After causing some deaths there, it strengthened in the Gulf of Mexico. On the morning of August 29, 2005, in southeast Louisiana and at the Louisiana-Mississippi state line, the storm called Katrina became a Category 3 hurricane. At least 1,836 people lost their lives in Hurricane Katrina and in the subsequent floods, making it the deadliest U.S. hurricane since the Okeechobee hurricane that struck the Leeward Islands, Puerto Rico, the Bahamas, and Florida in September of 1928.

These events took place all over the world, at different times, in different seasons, affecting different races and classes of people, and yet nobody was immune to the upset. No survivor went unscathed by the deafening aftermath—soaring rates of suicide, inconsolable grief, guilt, and despair. Every person touched by the nightmare faced the sobering reality of his or her own mortality and was tormented by the cruel realization that we are finite and vulnerable to forces that are more powerful than we are—forces of good, evil, natural, and unnatural.

Tragedy levels the field. When faced with the paralyzing magnitude of disasters like these, we unite. We weep in unison. We console in concert. We pray in one accord. And together we question what God allows.

We cry from the depths of our souls, "*Abba, Father*," while needing to know direction and how to get a grip on a life that has suddenly slipped away. We ask why. We ask how. We ask why again.

I believe that there is nothing inherently wrong with asking questions. Looking for answers is the beginning of sound understanding. But in the midst of tragedy and duress, our tendency is to question from a place of bitterness and anger, rather than with a pure and humbled heart. Consequently, our prayers begin to change directions. They move from questioning with a tone of faith to questioning with a tone of indifference to God and superiority to His will.

A few months ago, after I'd spent a good deal of time being on the road and beyond busy with speaking engagements, my son Eliot's college preparations, writing books, and everything else that came my way, October rolled in and all the busyness stopped. I ended up alone one night with no cable connection, no cell phone signal, and nothing to do but think.

> In the midst of tragedy and duress, our tendency is to question from a place of bitterness and anger.

What you should know about me is that God's mercies truly are renewed in my life every morning.

It takes all of that to keep me from dwelling on past mistakes or gripping meandering bitterness and pain left from, say, a terrorist attack. Each day, in my quiet time with my Father, my efforts are to present my emotions and my questions to Him so that He might show them to me relative to the grand scheme of things. Why? So I can loosen the grip I have on my misery.

But lately I've been noticing more of my imperfections and my resistance to life and God's will. I have noticed my train of thought changing direction.

It has come to my attention that I've somehow fallen into

the habit of, or should I say that I've fallen victim to, relying on my own understanding and praying for those things that I believe to be best for the world, rather than asking for God's will to be done. Consequently, my requests to Him have been merely efforts to persuade Him to repent His own will and to do things my way. For all intents and purposes, it seems that I've decided that the ideas of strength and faith beyond weakness (see Joshua 1:6-9), growing and learning through pain (see Romans 5:1-5), and all things working for good (see Romans 8:28) are not quite comfort enough for all that ails the world . . . or me.

At first glance, I'm sure that my saying this does not present a pretty picture of a woman of faith, who claims to love God more than anything else and to trust His Word above all.

"Father, I believe. Help my unbelief."

But there are questions and situations that happen in life that are so much bigger than me that they demand a word bigger than *faith*. They demand an explanation grander than a simple surrender to all the "bad" that God allows.

Mine is a simple mind. Most of the time, it takes me a little while to process a thought and assign meaning to it. And so, that October night when all the busyness stopped and I was alone with nothing to do but think, I processed.

I processed, and for the first time in my life, I could see that we are bigger than our questions. We are bigger than our inabilities to understand the mind of God and His power.

> We have created for ourselves the image of a selfish and vain god who needs us to praise Him for His glory.

I believe that we have misinterpreted what it means to refer to the sovereignty of God. And we have created for ourselves the image of a selfish and vain god who needs us to praise Him for His glory. This god has no real interest in us and does exactly as he pleases, in spite of us, allowing our pain and suffering as punishment for disobedience. We feel we must beg him to be kind to us and quietly offer up the fact that "god is in control" as consolation for our suffering. How can we expect to love such a god? As extreme as it may sound in writing, how true it is that we do not fully trust God because we cannot fully understand His power.

This is what I know: *God is bigger than our limited understanding.* If we would start from the ground and work our way up, we would see that, first and foremost, we belong to God, our Father who loves us and has created all things for our pleasure and comfort. The original intent was a garden stoop, peaceful meals, and long talks at sunset.

God is bigger than our transgression. Despite our disobedience and evil choices, our Father designed a way to prevent the eternal damage done by the wickedness we hand out toward one another, the damage we have caused to the earth, and the insolence that is its consequence. He has caused all the pain in life to be life-giving that we might grow and gather strength from it to endure until the end.

God is bigger than our weaknesses. We must live with the tragedies. None of us is out of their reach, and each of us must live in expectation of them. We will remember the upsets, and we will forever know the fear that we felt when the cancer struck, when the rains came, or when the first plane hit. We will recall the look on a loved one's face as he or she passed into eternity. No matter the situation, we'll always remember the mazelike feelings and the confusion when the busyness stopped.

God is bigger than our pain. Nothing in life is so big that it goes beyond God's ability to redeem us to Himself and restore our lives. We are released from needing existential theory, purpose, or design.

God is bigger than life. Truth is, we really don't have the wherewithal to understand all the whys and hows in life. We need only believe that He is more massive than all of our explanations of situations, and even the situations themselves. We need only to stand tall when the strong winds blow and life leaves us weak and afraid. We need only to believe that He knows and seeks to heal our pain, and as we mutter through life, experiencing the good and the bad, *we must believe that He is bigger.*

That's all I have, really. That's the best I can do. I admit that I don't understand all of the man-made whys or hows of life and tragedy any more than you do, but I have traded "understanding" for the knowledge that there is One greater than me who does understand it all, and I trust Him! I trust Him to be unchanging— constant, with us through it all, providing the miracles that allow some things to be unexplainable now and revealed in the fullness of time.

> I have traded "understanding" for the knowledge that there is One greater than me who does understand it all, and I trust Him!

I trust Him to provide the answers that I need right now and to do all things necessary to redeem lost mankind to Himself. I trust Him not to change the world according to the gospel of Leslie but according to His perfection! His Sovereignty!

Bless the Lord, O my soul!

As long as we live, life will keep happening. There will be disasters, distress, and things that are enormous in impact. But there is something about faith, something about the person of God, something about trusting Him that feels right, even in the middle of chaos. There is something about His consistency and His redemptive design that somehow lines it all up in the grand scheme of things, and He comes out bigger than our doubts, bigger than our sins, bigger than our disasters, and bigger than life.

The sixth chapter of Isaiah describes the enormity of our Father's presence.

In the year that King Uzziah died, I saw the Lord seated on a throne, high and exalted, and the train of his robe filled the temple. Above him were seraphs, each with six wings: With two wings they covered their faces, with two they covered their feet, and with two they were flying. And they were calling to one another:

"Holy, holy, holy is the LORD Almighty;
    the whole earth is full of his glory."

At the sound of their voices the doorposts and thresholds shook and the temple was filled with smoke. (Isaiah 6:1-4)

What's bigger than that?

No one ever told me that grief felt so like fear. The same fluttering in the stomach, the same restlessness. I keep on swallowing.

—C.S. Lewis, *A Grief Observed*

CHAPTER 3

THE LOSS OF A LOVED ONE

Beauty for Ashes

Over the last few months, I have collected letters, gifts, and cards from a number of people who have read *Between Heaven and Ground Zero*. The book moved their hearts and prompted them to share their stories with me. The letters speak of intense personal pain, loss, and the difficulty of getting past the grief.

One letter from a young man who lost his mother said that he hurt on so many levels that he felt like a different person on the inside—someone very different from what he showed on the outside. Another, from a wife who lost everything after her husband died on 9-11, said that she couldn't decide which death hit her hardest, her husband's or that of her old life.

Although I was moved by every letter that I received, one in particular—from a woman who had to sign a Do Not Resuscitate order for her eight-year-old son—sent chills down my spine. She sent me a blanket and a picture of him in his tiny casket.

I am worn out from groaning; all night long I flood my
bed with weeping and drench my couch with tears.
(Psalm 6:6)

These are just a few of the many stories that exist out there in my world . . . and likely yours. It's heartbreaking to know that people are suffering on so many levels, crying and longing for relief from the pain of incredible loss. The grief for some is unrelenting.

When someone close to us dies, we experience that loss on many levels. Not only are we faced with the physical loss, but we also face the loss of potential, what could have been. We miss the person's presence. We long to experience their smell again, how they laughed, how they were when they watched their favorite movie. We wish for the good old days and additional time to make each moment more meaningful.

The sudden realization that life is fleeting is sobering. The preoccupation with fantasies involving what life would have been like had that person lived becomes a silent driving force behind our days.

Whether the loss is sudden—we received a 2:00 a.m. phone call with the tragic news—or we shared our loved one's final moments of a long illness, the initial shock and grief seem endless. It doesn't matter how prepared we are or aren't. A loved one's death always leaves us feeling numb and disoriented.

When my mother died, my family stopped living for a long

time. We'd sit around for hours and not know what to say to console each other. My father grieved deeply and kept wishing for his own death. He had no idea who he was without my mom.

A few years ago, my cousin Randy was robbed and murdered outside of his home in Chicago. The news of his sudden death sent shock waves through my family.

> It doesn't matter how prepared we are or aren't. A loved one's death always leaves us feeling numb and disoriented.

In every situation, well-meaning friends and associates gathered to offer help. Their kind words suggested that we trust God and let ourselves experience the grief process. They told us that our loved ones were in a better place and that we should rejoice for them, and then they suggested that was the way to heal.

While I appreciate every word and every prayer that went out for my family during those times, I understand now that grief is not linear. You don't "start" at the loss and then proceed in a nice, straight line through phases like "anger" or "sadness" or "depression" until you reach the "end" of the line and the end of the process. That would be nice if it were true, but God didn't make us that way, and grief does not follow any blueprint.

There will be good days and bad days and days when you're left wondering who you are without that person's definition in your life. You will feel broken and helpless and alone—as if you have lost part of yourself. You'll be afraid and then strong again, and without realizing it, you'll find yourself crying all over again.

The emotions that you feel now are probably more intense than anything you've ever felt in your life—and rightly so. Death is a very unpredictable, traumatic, and disruptive experience.

We spend most of our lives preparing to live, not to die. We expect our lives to be long and fulfilled and to match the promises of God, which is life in abundance. We forget, or on some level we choose to ignore, the fact that death is stage one of the two stages of life. Stage two is life itself, which is our eternity. Translation: For people of faith, this life is preparation for a greater life to come. Life will be better and more satisfying in the everlasting. Why then should we mourn such a time of celebration?

I realize that this knowledge might offer little comfort when you're in the midst of the unique pain of losing someone.

So I offer this: Grief is not only about the individual who has died, but also about the individual left behind. If I've come to believe anything after losing twenty-two friends in one day, both parents, and someone I loved very dearly, I believe that a significant portion of the grieving process we go through is not only because of the loss through death of the one we care about; it may also be for the death of part of who we are as well.

Certainly, I am not suggesting that grief is selfish in any way. Instead, I propose to you that perhaps our grief is as significant for us in mourning the loss of that part of us that our loved one defined as it is for mourning the loss of our loved one. Perhaps the understanding of what is going on in our hearts, why we are feeling what we are feeling, will somehow make it easier for our faith in God and the care of friends to help us return to the joys of living.

> To appoint unto them that mourn in Zion, to give unto them beauty for ashes, the oil of joy for mourning, the garment of praise for the spirit of heaviness; that they might be called trees of righteousness, the planting of the LORD, that he might be glorified. (Isaiah 61:3, KJV)

Maybe we can grasp the understanding that going forward with healing from grief doesn't mean forgetting about the person we've lost. Getting back to enjoying life doesn't mean that you no longer miss a loved one. How long it takes until you start to feel better isn't a measure of how much you loved the person. With time and God's grace, you can find ways to cope with even the deepest loss.

I suggest that you allow your faith to play its role through your grief. Be patient and find solace in knowing that God will lead you and give you the strength to live your life differently than before, without that person. Your life doesn't become smaller or less significant. It simply changes. You live, laugh, and enjoy life again.

> Getting back to enjoying life doesn't mean that you no longer miss a loved one.

For now, don't look for answers. Don't ask questions. Don't blame God or anyone else for your loss. Don't stifle your anger. Don't pretend it's okay. Don't believe that life won't happen without that person. And most of all, don't expect anything outside of Christ's promises of comfort and healing. Only He can make something beautiful from these ashes.

There is no prescription or course of action that will tell you exactly how He will do it, but rest assured, my friend, He will do it! Our ever-gracious and almighty Lord knows how to comfort His children. He will not leave you comfortless. Somewhere, deep in what seems to be an unending emotional quagmire of pain and distress, God will give you the strength to breathe again.

Approach Him with great expectation. Reach out in your spirit, grab the hem of His robe, and live.

Here's an exercise for you.

Grab two chairs and place them face-to-face. Sit in one chair, and imagine that God is in the other. Now talk to Him. Don't talk in a pattern, as you are likely to do when you pray. Talk more as if you were talking to a friend, just as you would anyone else. Tell Him exactly how you are feeling about your loss. Explain to Him what your fears are. Tell Him about the best memories that you shared with your loved one. Now ask Him to take care of that person until you meet with that person again. Ask God to kiss your loved one for you and tell him or her that you will be okay. Now grab Him around His waist, cry your eyes out, and then . . . let go. Now, let Him hold you.

> *Heavenly Father,*
>
> *Only You can mend a broken heart and make beauty from the ashes of our losses. My sister or my brother needs You right now to be real for them. They need Your comfort, and they need to begin to feel alive again. Breathe now, Holy Spirit, new life and resurrection. Breathe healing and make Your presence known. Bring comfort as only You can, by whatever means necessary.*
>
> *We ask that those watching might come to know the unsurpassed mercy and grace of our Lord Jesus Christ.*
> *Amen.*

CHAPTER 4

DETOUR

I Want My Life Back

Once upon a time in Leslie Land, I would get out of bed every morning and complain about having to get out of bed every morning. With my eyes half opened, I'd mutter about in the kitchen, making my coffee and glancing out the window at the peek of sunlight. I'd inhale the beautiful fresh morning air with no mindful thought of the blessings I'd been given, and I'd complain.

I complained about being single. I complained about my career, my car, my neighbors, my family, my friends or lack thereof, my health, and even my wardrobe. Then, as you already know, one beautiful September morning changed everything. The day stopped the noise.

Once upon a time in your life, you most likely went about your ordinary, every day breathing clean air and complaining about something. Your earth was not moving with any great events either, and like me, you probably muttered about your daily life, complaining about the humdrum of the common and the ordinary. You probably dreamed about what life could be like, what things and people should be like, and what would make life more exciting for you. You thought that the grass was greener in the neighbor's yard.

Then, suddenly, and without warning, your earth quaked— divorce, cancer, AIDS, Katrina, Bin Laden, Sri Lanka, drug overdose, kidnapping, child molestation—and all the mutterings stopped.

For one quick and very surreal moment, you inhaled, and then you stopped breathing. Winded by the sudden movement in your universe and paralyzed by the attention that it demanded, you stood motionless, suspended in time, caught off guard, and dizzied by its final collapse.

Your face froze. Your hands were wet and your eyes fixed on some gruesome sight that would later become the center of your pain. A previously vague odor burned itself through your nostrils. Life was derailed. Suddenly, it was foul air you breathed, and your once humdrum, ordinary life took a detour down a path that landed you headfirst into a huge pile of madness. Desperately you argued the postscript that life as you knew it only seconds before this colossal moment in time, was over. The journey to recovery and healing would be an internal one.

I penned this little story to better illustrate my point.

CHRISTMAS 1896

The Christmas trees on our lane were beautifully adorned with the magic of the season. The carolers, dressed in long, flowing gowns and neatly tied white bonnets, wandered up and down the road, singing all the usual songs of merriment and seasonal joy. I often watched the women, amused by the long trails their dresses left behind in the snow. I loved this time of year, with its ringing bells and the smell of roasted bird and plum pudding saturating the air around me.

Husband, which is what I called my husband, was twenty-six years old that year. I was twenty-two. He was a designer by trade and thus always dressed himself in the finest wardrobe and silk scarves. I'd sometimes walk behind him to get a scent of his oils. Husband was a distinguished young man, to say the least.

He was strikingly handsome, and very tall, even to tall men—more than six and a half feet, I'd say. He had a very strong chin and a strong countenance . . . stern eyes, a very prominent nose, and the whimsical smile of a small boy. This, I believe, is what attracted me to him.

Me, well, it's no matter what I'm like, except to say that Husband often described me as being "all he never knew he wanted." And so our lives were perfect, until this one particular night of our perfection.

It was Christmas Eve, and Husband and I decided to settle in early on this night of miracles. We sat quietly by the fire and offered love to our Savior in celebration of His birth. I made a nice rum punch, and Husband brought warm chestnuts to the table. "A book would be nice," he said to me. "Oh yes," I responded. We decided on Christie's Christmas. A simple story, but a favorite in our home nonetheless.

I sat in my chair near the front of the fireplace at Husband's feet and took inventory of our festive home. It was beauty from every angle. A crackling fire burned brightly in the fireplace with fresh logs, giving plenty of heat and ambiance. Hanging from the mantle were my old stockings that Husband and I had painted by hand with our special oils, then filled with candies and Christmas treats. On the mantle were the Christmas candles that were almost gone, as we'd burned them each year of our two-year union.

Homemade paper tinsel hung near the windows. It glowed in a warm myriad of glorious colors under the lights from the candles. And our tree, which stood boldly to the right of the fire-place, held our ornamental memories of Christmases past. Indeed, we'd decked our halls with Christmas joy and seasonal beauty.

The room was beautiful from every angle.

Just then, my inventory was interrupted when movement caught my eyes. Husband put down his rum punch on the stoop in front of the fire, picked up the book, and took his place to the left of me. "Are you ready, my love?" he asked.

Flickers of feathered tinsel glided back and forth, moving closer to the ground and to where Husband's glass sat. Then suddenly, everything was out of place. Fire engulfed the room. Heat exploded throughout my body, and all was dark and quiet for me.

I was all he never knew he wanted. Husband lived to be eighty-one. He never remarried, never really loved again, and never regained his life.[1]

Fast forward to your life and mine.

Life can change directions in an instant. In the blink of an eye, it can become more than a challenge to wake up every day; no days are good days anymore, and the only active thought in your brain is the burning question, *What now?*

What now, indeed, as perhaps the most ambiguous points in the journey begin—accepting the loss of life, dealing with the anger at what life has become, forgiving yourself for being alive, and then making the decision to live. This is what you must do.

Truth is, even though life has been radically altered and these next days, months, or even years will quite possibly hold the most difficult burdens you've ever had to bear, it is doable.

You will survive.

God gives us the promise that He has already kept. Isaiah 53 says

> He is despised and rejected by men,
>> A Man of sorrows and acquainted with grief.
>> And we hid, as it were, our faces from Him;
>> He was despised, and we did not esteem Him.
>> Surely He has borne our griefs,
>> And carried our sorrows;
>> Yet we esteemed Him stricken,
>> Smitten by God, and afflicted.
>> But He was wounded for our transgressions,
>> He was bruised for our iniquities;
>> The chastisement for our peace was upon Him,
>> And by His stripes we are healed. (Isaiah 53:3-5, NKJV)

You will survive.

You will live the promise and make the decision to keep your life in motion, get back on your feet again, and return to the land of the living. You will want to breathe again, and you will breathe. You will want to wake up again to an open window and an equally wide-open future. You will want life.

I propose to you that even in this life, there is life after death.

At this point, I wish I could offer some great spiritual insight or anecdote to drive home the points I've made, winding them up by telling you exactly what to do and how to regain your sense of security and self-assurance. But I believe the better way is to actually lose them both and then redefine yourself in light of who God is and your relationship to Him.

I wish there were some words of comfort that I could share,

outside of the infamous "if it happened, it's because it was God's will." Because, unfortunately, I don't believe that. I don't believe that God chooses the trauma in our lives. I believe that most of the pains we endure are consequences of the choices we make, or the choices made by others, and He is faithful and just in allowing us to live through those consequences. Through it all, however, I believe that He offers wide-open arms of consolation and a faultless plan to utilize our pain.

> I don't believe that God chooses the trauma in our lives.

You see, those of us who have smelled the stench of death's breath or inhaled the foul air of a hurricane; those of us whose bodies have been invaded by cancer and then suffocated by hopelessness are not consoled by simple words. Somewhere in the trenches of our darkness is a glimmer of inclination—no, *need*—no, somewhere in the trenches of our darkness is the *desperation* to find something real enough to fuel our survival.

Although pain has been our constant companion since the sin of the first Adam, I believe that deep within our collective DNA is memory of the perfect garden stoop, where we once sat and communed with our Creator and pain was nonexistent. I believe that somewhere deep in the soul of man rests the knowledge that life was never meant to take us so far from that stoop and so intimately close to pain. Somewhere, even amid the darkness of suffering, we still seek the light of recovery.

I believe that God has worked all things together for that purpose, that we might know life in the everlasting. I believe in a divine point of grace and a plan of redemption. I believe that Jesus Christ by His blood makes it possible for us to claim the lives He originally intended for us. I believe that life was meant to be good. It was meant to be filled with joy. We were never intended to live in the shadow of death or under the shroud of sin. We should, therefore, not look to getting back to where we were, but we should seek to move beyond it.

Jeremiah 29:11 says, "For I know the plans I have for you . . . plans to prosper you and not to harm you, plans to give you hope and a future." Plans to give you hope *and* a future.

As for me, I cried for months, yelling at God and demanding to have my life back. I prayed and shouted at Him and stumbled around in the darkness for months looking for that inclination, that glimmer of light. Then, one day, by the grace of God and a tiny miracle that He sent my way, I fell into His arms—and into my healing.

> I believe that life was meant to be good. It was meant to be filled with joy.

Who knows, maybe you, too, should fall . . .

Heavenly Father, our lives have spun out of control, and we don't know where to begin even looking for the pieces, least of all putting them back in place. Help us to understand that Your will for us is that we grow beyond what once was. Father, help us to see that Your plans are to prosper us beyond the temporal things of this world. Your plan is for our everlasting. Thank You for Your perfect plan, Father.
> *Amen.*

In the world you will have tribulation;
but be of good cheer, I have overcome the
world.

—Jesus (John 16:33, nkjv)

CHAPTER 5

WHAT NOW?

Miles to Go before I Sleep

*It's a normal evening run—until I hear heavy, familiar footsteps
behind me and bated breath creeping closer.*

It's him again. I just know it.

*I don't waste time looking around. Suddenly I remember
his cold hands around my neck.*

*Moving faster now. I smell the beer on his breath and the
faint scent of his cheap cologne. Could this be happening again?*

*Breathing deeper now and holding back tears, I pick up the
pace. My heart is pounding in my chest and threatening to explode,
as if it's daring me to keep going at this speed. But the images of*

his face—those eyes—keep me moving as they play over and over again in my head as fast as I am running, running, running, and making my way through the nearly darkened family park.

Each step is deliberate—running. Every forward movement is a task—still running. Almost faint by now—but still running. My thighs burn as I struggle to pick up the pace even more. A heavy tenor voice calls out from behind me through quick pants. "Stop running."

It's him.

His breathing is labored. His voice lands on the back of my neck. His breath is hot, agonizing.

I wince, running faster and crying now—no time to pray. My mind does a quick scan of the universe in search for God. How? Again?

He's running faster.

I'm running faster, almost not breathing at all now, but still running. Without thinking, without seeing—moving forward, pushing, running, determined not to let the footsteps behind me land another "boom" closer to me.

Running, running, running, and remembering his cold hands around my neck—his hot spit in my face. My legs are heavy. I'm dragging them.

He is so close behind me now that I am completely panicked. I reach my arms out in front of me—running—grab air, and use it to propel myself forward, not to breathe but to escape. Dragging every inch of me over to the clearing of the park toward home; determined not to feel his sweat touch my skin—again; panting. Just a few more feet into the wide open, I turn my head slightly to glance over my shoulder. I need to make sure he's not close.

My eyes meet his, his arms reach for me, the pillow covers my face, and I fall out of bed. . . .

Still running . . . ten years into my recovery . . . and I'm still running.[1]

Oscar Wilde once said that life imitates art far more than art imitates life. I'm not sure exactly how true that is, but I do believe that we expect a lot from our art. We expect our music to heal us and bring us peace, our paintings to reveal our hearts and answer the questions of life, and our writings to contain in them some profound words that inspire and motivate us beyond our situations and circumstances.

When a poet dies, he leaves behind a space of ambiguity—so many things unexplained and so many words unspoken. When a survivor wakes from the nightmare of that poetic loss and her particular tragedy, she steps into the certainty of static, hard work. Survival is profound, and it is every day.

Traumatic experiences upset our world like nothing else. They shake the very foundation of our belief system and everything we have come to regard as normal. It's impossible to describe what it looks like when normalcy all falls down. Not much is more difficult than leaving those pieces where they fall while maneuvering through the recovery expectations that we place on ourselves, the "hopes" that our loved ones have for us, and the prayers of the saints. Again, we expect a lot from our art.

I remember the first day of my therapy. I was a mess. My therapist came to my home because I was afraid to go out. When she arrived, she sat in the living room and quietly waited. It was about fifteen minutes before I had courage enough to join her. I walked into my living room where she was waiting. I was trying very hard to give the appearance of normal . . . whatever that looked like. I sat next to her, fully expecting to find out what Post-Traumatic Stress Disorder (PTSD) was, what it looked like, and how it would affect my life. Strangely enough, I remember exactly what I looked like on that day. I was wearing bald jeans and a blue T-shirt, and my hair was a mess.

Over the next few months, I learned more about my diagnosis and the medications I was taking. I learned that there were three main symptom clusters of PTSD, and I suffered from all of them. My case was severe. For months, I endured what are called "intrusions," flashbacks or nightmares where I experienced the traumatic events repeatedly. I suffered from avoidance and hyperarousal, which is increased arousal responses such as hypervigilance or increased startle response and withdrawal.

It was not unusual for me to relive the attack even when I tried to have a normal day. If I heard a car backfire or a door slam shut, if my dogs barked or a horn blew, I would all but jump out of my skin and drift off back to September 11.

While my reactions were immediate and obvious, it is important to note that not everyone reacts the way I did. Not everyone suffers from the same symptoms or in the same way that I did. There are no standard patterns of reaction to traumatic experiences. Each person is individual, and each reaction is as well.

The *Diagnostic and Statistical Manual of Mental Disorders* explains that symptoms vary and that it is possible for individuals to experience traumatic stress without manifesting PTSD. Some people show symptoms immediately, while others have delayed reactions. Some have adverse effects for a long period, while others recover rather quickly.

Understanding your individual and normal responses to these very abnormal events can help you to cope effectively with your feelings, thoughts, and behaviors. Knowing what to expect is a very important step along the path to recovery and healing.

I've listed a few of the more familiar reactions here for your reference.

DENIAL

There is usually an immediate disconnect that happens when tragedy strikes. My therapist explained to me that it's the brain's only means of defense, its way of protecting us. It's primal. Most victims will experience a disconnect or denial before they become survivors.

Denial is the coping mechanism that the brain uses to allow our mind the time it needs to adjust to the reality of what has happened. This stage might last just a few minutes, a few days, a few weeks, or longer. As with all of the grief stages, you might find yourself in and out of this stage at different times. The key is to understand that it's okay, as long as you are working through the trauma.

SHOCK AND NUMBNESS

At first, you might be in a state of shock, feeling numb and confused. You also might feel detached, as if what is happening isn't really happening, almost like watching a movie. For months, I felt numb. Much like denial, this is another coping mechanism for the brain. Again, it's okay. Just keep moving through the trauma.

DISSOCIATION

Daydreams that interfere with the ability to function can be another reaction to the trauma. This reaction is dysfunctional, a way to escape or deny the pain. Indications of dissociating include the body becoming stiff or still, missing conversations, and feeling like one is watching things from outside of the body.

FEAR, ANXIETY, AND PANIC

Crime shatters normal feelings of security and trust and the sense of control. Fear, anxiety, and panic often go hand in hand in creating the unbalance that you will likely feel, so expect to be afraid and insecure. Your entire world, all that you found safety in, has just been altered, and you had no time to prepare for the upset. You might feel jumpy and nervous, like you are going crazy. Often, this feeling happens because traumatic disasters are so incomprehensible. Being anxious when you leave your home, being nervous when you are alone, being easily startled by loud or sudden noises, and being overcome by waves of panic are all signs that your body and mind are still reeling. I want to encourage you to hang in there. It really does get better. Remember that healing takes time. Though it might seem like each day endures forever, these feelings will go away or lessen. Your healing will come.

INTENSE EMOTION

Your heart will certainly break. But you might also feel crushed by sadness and cry uncontrollably. Try to remember that tears are healthy and cleansing. Don't hold them back. Holding it in can actually make the grieving process last longer. I cried all the time, not knowing that I was helping myself. It's good to know now.

GUILT

Most people who survive a tragic event or are injured in a traumatic disaster want to understand why the tragedy happened in the first place. However, the guilt and regret for things you did or did not do, things you said or did not say that should have or could have protected someone else are almost impossible to find answers for. It's a natural response to the guilt to find yourself thinking, "If only I had . . . " My advice: Don't go there. You're not more powerful than almighty God. There is nothing you could have done.

> Recognize and respect the anger as being real, but don't use it as an excuse to abuse or hurt others.

ANGER

It is natural for you to be angry and outraged at the tragedy, the person who caused the tragedy, or someone you believe could have prevented it. You might even get angry with God. You might daydream or have dreams about revenge. These feelings are not right or wrong; they are a natural part of the recovery process, and they are just feelings. Recognize and respect the anger as being real, but don't use it as an excuse to abuse or hurt others.

Personally, anger was a big deal for me. I had a recurring dream about 9-11. I dreamed that I was back in the building, running through all the floors blowing a horn and warning people of the danger. I lowered a rope from one of the top floors down to the street and guided people down to safety.

Every time I had that dream, I woke up in a cold sweat, shivering, crying, and not willing to admit that I was angry, but I was. I was angry with God and with everyone else. Initially, this is what my anger looked like. I wrote this early one morning after not sleeping for a few days.

I was strong until you came
You kissed me with your new ideas of religion and your
*   causes and called it martyrdom*
I called it rape
I was confident until you spoke
Your belligerence ran through me and curdled my blood
My sisters cried for me and colleagues died on my behalf,
*   and you said it was truth,*
But you lied
Evil birthed you, but I nurtured you
I fed your wives and raised your children
I supported your beliefs and fought for your rights to
*   have them,*
And you thanked me with visions of humanity colliding
*   with gravity*
And dreams of slaughtered twins soaked in dust and blood
*   and said it was justice*
I say it's sin
I was religious until you introduced me to your Allah, and
*   your words of wisdom joined hands with my friends and*
*   spattered the place where my children played*
You shouted victory from your mountains and caves, then

dared to put God's name in that black mouth you call
your country
I call it hell
I was hopeful until your soldiers invaded my skies and
shredded my plans with
Your delusions of an equality that severs goals with
shattered glass,
While the future rains down on a city like confetti
And you labeled this a holy war
But I know God
Mothers scream and children cry
And all the earth looks on, as brothers dig for fathers and
heroes search for badges
But as you sip your wine and watch the signs, still
claiming victory
I count seals
For the Lord God, Alpha and Omega
ELOHIM, Jehovah-Jireh is my Deliverer
But you'll call him "Judge"
You'll fall on your knees and declare, "I am"
You'll drink the blood of your lost ones, and your children
will know "I am"
You'll run to the rocks and find no hiding place
You'll look for your soldiers and they'll
be no more
Then you'll know terror
And I'll know righteousness!

Eventually, God placed it on my heart to forgive the entire nation of Islamic believers, and then to forgive myself. It came like a waterfall, with tears of compassion and a deep, heartfelt burden for souls. If you are experiencing the anger, know that God will soon set you free from it.

DEPRESSION AND LONELINESS

Depression and loneliness can be a big part of trauma for many survivors. It marks the breakdown of your defenses in times of grief. The reality of loss sinks in deeply and becomes a stage of grief with compounded symptoms of sadness and hopelessness, lack of interest, loss of appetite, sometimes thoughts of suicide, wishing to be dead, loss of interest in sex, difficulty concentrating, and feelings of worthlessness. Depression can be the most difficult stage to get through because it comes with so many other reactions. Don't face these feelings alone. Get help!

ISOLATION

Tragedy sets you apart from many people. Surviving natural or unnatural disasters is an abnormal occurrence, and people are afraid of it. The more extreme the trauma, the wider the gap will be. Having or surviving a fatal disease carries with it a stigma. The more apparent the suffering, the more people shy away. Each of these situations can leave you feeling abandoned and even ashamed. Try to remember that your situation is *not* unique, and you are *not* alone. God has not forgotten you. He really does love you, and He wants the best for your life. Try to believe.

PHYSICAL DISTRESS

Although not extremely common, it is not unusual to have migraines, persistent fatigue, nausea, sleeplessness, and weight gain or weight loss. Some people have even reported lower backaches, chills, sweats, and grinding teeth.

SOCIAL INADEQUACY

You might be unable to function in social settings. It might be hard to think and plan, and the things that used to be enjoyable might be meaningless. You might not be able to laugh, and when you finally do, you might feel guilty. Tears come often and without warning.

Mood swings, irritability, dreams, and flashbacks are common. Take your time. Travel this road at your own pace.

INSOMNIA

Because of difficulty in putting the incident out of mind, some people won't have any immediate reaction other than insomnia. It might be weeks or months before other symptoms surface. This type of delayed reaction is not unusual.

I bargained my way into a new life in Christ. Amen!

BARGAINING

This is probably the briefest of all the stages for most people, but it's normally the final effort to find some way to ease the pain. Bargaining simply seeks to trade some thing or some action with God to control life and make the pain go away. I finally agreed to get to know Him and allow Him to know me. I bargained my way into a new life in Christ. Amen!

Note that I created this list based on my own experience, lessons, and the little things that I discovered through therapy. It is in no way a comprehensive list, nor should it serve as a reference for treatment. If you are suffering in any way similar to what I describe here, please seek the professional help of a godly therapist.

As you progress in your personal journey of recovery toward healing, remember that there are no rules here, and there are no time restrictions in being symptomatic or being in recovery. There are no levels of wellness, and you should not compare what you feel to the feelings of others. Right now, it is what it is, and recovery means rebuilding trust with God first, then with others, and then with ourselves. Recovery is taking huge steps forward to relearn what is safe and what is human. During this time, if you're honest and open, you will gain a new perspective about life, and death will lose its sting.

You will gain the lost authenticity in being, peace in your

everyday life, and power for living. But this, my friend, is a journey, and there are miles to go before you can truly exhale.

In his poem "Stopping by Woods on a Snowy Evening," Robert Frost explains recovery perfectly. He says, "The woods are lovely, dark, and deep, But I have promises to keep, and miles to go before I sleep, and miles to go before I sleep. . . . "

A recovery journey is a journey through life in which we face our pain and fears with directed focus on the healing that is ahead. Without obsessing over results, we just keep living, remembering that we are aiming for stability, not perfection. We keep moving, with a directive of openness and peace. Recovery doesn't have to be hard. It doesn't have to send us into sessions of guilt and repetition, and it doesn't have to destroy our finances. There is hope on the other side of wherever you are right now. You will laugh again, dance again, and feel joy again.

My advice after six years of the journey and then a healing experience is for you to remind yourself every day that even though God makes the healing possible, the recovery belongs to you.

There is work to be done, and unfortunately, it doesn't end with a six-week treatment program or a twelve-step initiative. It doesn't go away in therapy sessions and small groups at church. Prepare yourself for the questions that you'll undoubtedly ask over and over again and the meanings that God will provide to you, which, by the way, you'll learn again and again.

> There is hope on the other side of wherever you are right now. You will laugh again, dance again, and feel joy again.

Steady yourself now for the miles to go before you know sleep again; late nights and crying through prayer, lost friends, revelations, and the subtle flows of emotions that will, at times, turn the tide toward torrents of your very own tears.

But take heart, my friends, in this lifelong commitment to openness and readiness to be constantly and consistently transformed by the grace of God. Our Father has provided us with grand little stories designed to inspire our journeys and encourage us through to the end, and you can never go back to who you were and where you were before your day of all days and night of all nights.

Why would you want to when so great an opportunity for healing, transformation, realness, and genuine intimacy with God awaits you?

Let me pray for us.

Sweet, gentle Father, as we cross the threshold of this day with all of our burdens and fears and nightmares and feelings of hopelessness, we commit them to Your cross. We commit ourselves to You, mind, body, spirit, and soul, and we ask for strength in our recovery efforts and healing in our lives. We ask for Your healing waters . . . that they would flow in us, through us, and around us, that we would be swept away in You. We commit our relationships and all of our goals to Your care. We ask for Your mercy and more grace in our lives and on our journey.

Amen.

CHAPTER 6

THE AWAKENING

Slowing Down to Move Forward

Even unto the everlasting. That's the goal in life. To live this unpredictable life journey through suffering, hoping, growing, and enduring until the end.

I understand that now, but for most of my life, I found it difficult to understand anything presented to me from any vantage point other than the immediacy of my own flesh. Either something was black or it was white, and whatever it was, it needed to be that, right then.

I even put God in that same box. I thought that He did all

that He was going to do in the immediate, or He did nothing at all. He was a God of right now, and even Scripture gave witness to that fact. *Now* faith is the substance. *Now* it came to pass. *Now* Jesus spoke.

It was just a few short years ago when my perspective changed. As I was going through therapy, I became so tired of what seemed to be an endless conversational loop about the stagnant misery of my life that I began to seek God for something more like His personality. I wanted huge, I wanted immediate, and I wanted unchanging.

I was not lost to what I needed. I knew that God was the key to my healing, so I felt myself in a distinct spiritual yearning. I wanted more of God, and I wanted Him right then. So much so that at times, my desire for Him made me cry aloud. I prayed, fasted, and begged for more of His presence in my life. I served and spoke in tongues and did every good deed that I could think of, all in a quest for immediate healing, more of God, and a place of spiritual favor.

Now, at first glance, you might think to say what a beautiful thing it is to long for God in that way. You might think me pious and of sound faith. However, at a second look, you will discover, just as I did, that something more substantial was missing. I did everything *but* take time to get to know the person of Jesus Christ. Full recovery, which is healing, only comes by way of the Cross.

Oftentimes in our quest to know the full flavor of God and His healing hand, we skip a beat. Most often in our desires to have it all right now, even in godly desires, we forsake the most critical component, that which takes the most time. We need to slow down in order to move forward.

For the first time in my life, I might have had an inclination of something significant beyond instant gratification.

But I didn't put the pieces together overnight. I didn't wake one morning to see a bright light of revelation flash before my eyes.

For months, I ran in circles, chasing my tail, working hard to no avail. I just kept pushing, chasing, and getting more and more discouraged by the lack of results. I spent a lot of days crying and a lot of nights being sick from crying all day. I went back and forth emotionally. One day I was okay and the next I was back to thinking I was worthless and wanting to die. One day I was calm and the next day I was in constant panic mode. I even had times when I was so angry with God that I shouted at Him from a very bitter heart.

Pause.

I believe that, contrary to what we've been taught, God is not threatened by our anguished cries or our troubled thoughts. Even though He may not answer immediately, He will never abandon us or use emotional blackmail when we are honest about our pain. In Psalm 7:6, David tells God to wake up. God Himself referred to David as a man after God's heart.

> God is not threatened by our anguished cries or our troubled thoughts.

Getting back on track . . .

I kept shouting and crying until eventually I noticed that between the cries I was learning to trust God with the honesty of what I was really feeling. I wasn't just giving Him "good Christian answers" anymore. He was getting Leslie. I think that's about the time I started falling in love and began hearing His voice.

Here's what I was told. God does not desire only recovery for our lives. He desires to heal us. Healing is an active process that returns us to the wholeness of life that was lost. It encompasses our whole self—the heart and the spirit . . . and it takes time. Jesus assures us that He will heal us, not always as we may wish, but always with new faith that gives us hope.

> God does not desire only recovery for our lives. He desires to heal us.

I learned that it was okay to *not* be okay. Even more, I learned that it was okay to take my time and enjoy the healing comforts of my Father's arms.

Then somewhere in the middle of my agony, I began to notice a growing relationship with God my Father, and in that relationship, healing was happening to me . . . for me . . . around me . . . in me. My Best Friend and Confidant stayed near me in my moments of insecurity. My Lovely and Beloved was each day giving me a gift that allowed me to stay open in order that He could repair that which was broken.

Because of His gentle care, I never noticed that the clock kept ticking. I forgot to notice that time was passing. But it was. What had once been an open and bleeding wound and was now scabbed over with anger, fear, resentment, disappointment, unbelief, bitterness, loneliness, depression, guilt, doubt, and feeling alone . . . pause here and really hear me . . . was becoming softer to the touch. But again, it was His touch.

Six years later, here I am, still getting softer to His touch. I don't shout as much as I did when we first started seeing each other, and daily now, I forgive myself a little more for being human and for taking so much time to heal. I must admit, however, I'm loving the journey. I have loved each and every one of the 2,629,743.83 minutes that I've spent so far being in this relationship and being touched by Him.

Speaking of being touched . . .

Father, be for me and for my friends also, the continual healing of our mind, body, spirit, and soul, averting everything contrary to that result. Open our hearts, and replace the pain that You find there with Your peace, unshakable faith, authentic love, wisdom, and sobriety in how we view our healing journeys. Slow us down, Father, if it be Your will. Open the eyes of our hearts, for Your glory, that we might live preserved in Your holiness even unto everlasting. Amen.

CHAPTER 7

PERFECT GIFTS

Grace Flows Down

"*Tanya?*" *Momma called from the kitchen.*

"*Yes.*" *Tanya's voice chimed over the blaring stereo. It was a typical teenage annoyance to be disturbed while the music was playing. Some type of unspoken but well-known law.*

"*I need you to take a drive to Mother Phelps' house and pick up a package for me.*"

Tanya sucked the air through her teeth. "You don't mean right now, do you?"

"*Yes, Tanya, I do mean right now.*"

"*Right now?*"

"*Yes, Tanya. Now!*"

"*Right this very minute now?*"

Tanya heard her mother slam the oven door shut, and as her footsteps neared the stairs, Tanya called out to her.

"*But it's raining outside, and you know how Daddy hates for me to drive in the rain. Besides, I'm still doing my homework, and you know how you hate it when I don't finish what I start.*"

"*Tanya, I can hear the music blaring from all the way down here. So what class is it you're doing homework in . . . is it 'hip-hop math' or 'dancing with chemistry'? Tanya, dear, just go," Mother told her.*

The rain was only a faint drizzle. Tanya looked outside the window and tried to find one last reason she could use to stay home. She found none.

It wasn't really going that she didn't like. It was Mother Phelps.

Mother Phelps was at least ninety years old with sharp, pointy teeth. Her white hair was unusually long, held together by a strong twisted braid that lay flat down her back. She was always asking if it was coming loose. The joke among the kids at church was that she was so old that her body was made from the original dust of the earth.

Mother Phelps was a mean, surly, and cantankerous old lady with a raspy old voice. She never had anything nice to say, ever, to anyone. She just sat in the same old wheelchair by her window, day after day, smelling of mothballs and Chanel No. 5 and cussing at passersby. None of the kids in church could stand to be around her for any length of time, especially Tanya, who was particularly sensitive to smells. Therefore, she whined one last time before leaving the house.

"*Mom, are you sure this can't wait for Dad?" Silence.*

Legend was that back in the day, Mother Phelps was a bootlegger (among other things). She'd hosted wild parties that lasted until the wee hours of the morning. And in her heyday, she was the toast of the town.

But the Mother Phelps Tanya knew lived in the same old house, which was the oldest house in town. A landmark, it sat in the middle of Main Street, right in the center of town. The floors creaked, the windows were dressed with thick drapes year-round, and Mother Phelps had twelve cats, all named Stanley.

Tanya walked slowly to her dresser and turned the stereo off. She packed her books, finished putting them away, and called out again to her mother. "Mom, did Mother Phelps say exactly what it is that I'm supposed to be picking up? Can I just run in and run out?"

Tanya had often picked up a simple list of things that Mother Phelps needed from the store. Other times, she would accompany her mother to Mother Phelps's home, where she and her mom would clean, cook, and even give Mother Phelps a bath. Tanya dreaded those types of visits. She was glad that this would at least not be one of those.

Tanya bounced down the stairs as she normally did and toward the kitchen where Momma was obviously still preparing dinner.

The sound of her sneakers made little dull thuds when they struck the carpet on the stairs. Tanya enjoyed trying to make a beat from it. As her foot hit the final step, her heart exploded.

And so did something from the kitchen. A pop and a bang and a snap happened at the same time. There was a moan and then a thud, all individual and yet indivisible. There was a glimpse of the back of a man's head running from the back door, and there was Mom, on the kitchen floor, moving very slowly in a growing stream of blood from her back.

> *Mom looked at Tanya and smiled through her pain. She reached for her daughter's trembling hand and said in a very calm and quiet voice, "It's okay, Baby Girl. God has me."*[1]

Why do bad things happen to good people?

In my lifetime, I've heard that question asked at least a trillion times. Every time I've heard it, it's resonated inside my head. Having faced my own mortality, and after having lived so much of life without God as my center, there has been an occasion or two when I've asked it myself.

Truth is, we've all wondered at some point or another about justice and purpose. We've all questioned God's mercy when seeing the frail bones of a child dying of starvation in Africa, or hearing of a devoted mother losing her entire family in a car accident. We've all speculated that perhaps God is snoozing. We've wondered if by chance there isn't some obstinate force working behind the scenes to ruin life in general, and we're all really just unsuspecting pawns in a hostile universe.

But it's normal to try to find reason and understanding. Our hearts break in the light of tragedy, and we want to make things right, or at the very least explain them. It's perfectly human to desire an understanding of why the innocent suffer. Our faith is challenged when our lives spiral out of control, and we want to know the mind of God relative to tragedy. We need to believe that He cares.

> It's perfectly human to desire an understanding of why the innocent suffer.

And so, ours is the tendency to rationalize in order to make things more bearable. Some approach our situations from a super-spiritual perspective, blending universal belief with God's promises for an all-encompassing rule of cause and effect, which answers all the whys for all circumstances and every occasion. Just add faith and stir.

The result is faith adages that even sound like Bible verses: "God helps those who help themselves." "Cursed is the one who trusts in man, who depends on flesh for his strength, and whose heart turns away from the Lord." And my personal favorite, "God takes care of babies and fools."

We have successfully created for ourselves neat and brilliant little quick hits that we use when all else fails. They contain in them the secret to a good life and justification for why tragedy happens, reduced to what goes around, comes around. Translation: If you work hard, keep your nose clean, and raise a "good" family, you'll enjoy good health and happiness until you die in a peaceful sleep at a ripe old age.

We fail to realize that while these man-made rules of thumb offer immediate gratification on most fronts, they eliminate the need for grace and replace faith in God's promises with the guarantee of a life equation: Sin equals suffering, and morality then equals prosperity. Period. So then, with scissors in hand, we run madly through life, proclaiming our entitlement to carve out our own happiness and being offended when tragedy strikes.

September 11 was not the first time, nor will it be the last time, that we asked questions. We asked when the tsunami struck South Asia in 2004 and when Hurricane Katrina devastated New Orleans in 2005; and we ask indefatigably when tragedy takes a face and becomes intimately personal.

We forget that life is a series of actions, consequences, and results that produce life events. And whether they be by God's hand or ours, being moral will not always equal prosperity. Sometimes in this life, morality will partner with righteousness and equal suffering. But God's plan is redemptive.

> Sometimes in this life, morality will partner with righteousness and equal suffering.

Before man disobeyed God in the Garden, he experienced peace with God, himself, his companion, and all of God's creation.

Sin broke those relationships on all levels and changed the way life works. God's plan restores order. It brings healing to all these relationships and does not depend on our morality or goodness. It depends on His mercy and His grace.

In August of 2002, a woman in our church named Chandra saw her only son, Suresh, off to Iraq to fight for our country. She and her husband, Jeff, felt a little concerned about Suresh going, but they supported his decision. The church supported them all. In October, Jeff fell ill suddenly and went into a coma. Because his prognosis was not good, the military allowed Suresh a temporary leave so that he could be at his father's side when he passed. Jeff died the day before Suresh arrived.

Both Chandra and Suresh were devastated. The church rallied near the family and prayed for their peace and strength. Things got better slowly, but we all knew that because this death was unexpected, it would be a long journey to healing.

One year later, the military granted Suresh another leave to visit with his mom. It was their first holiday season without Jeff. Chandra was still mourning and still reeling from the shock of her husband's death when, out of nowhere, one week before Christmas, a truck crossed the divider and killed her only son.

What words can be used to console such sorrow? What kind of love mends wounds so deep and a loss of faith so great? In the massive emptiness where answers to questions like *Why me?* become the only dialogue, how do we comfort? I think that in times of tragedy, whether we ask out loud or not, we all wonder exactly what grace is and where it can be found.

> In times of tragedy, whether we ask out loud or not, we all wonder exactly what grace is and where it can be found.

Many of us immediately look to the Word of God for answers, finding only temporary solace in hearing that God is in control and that nothing in all creation is hidden from God's sight. "Everything is uncovered and laid bare before the eyes of him to whom we must give account" (Hebrews 4:13). But that quickly fades under the pressure of ever-flowing tears.

Our pain demands answers. Whether tragedy comes to us through natural disasters, accidents, human error, or the wickedness of humanity, the question "Why do bad things happen to good people?" is thrown down like a gauntlet. It is intended to be the final word in the debate over God's power, His love for us, and even His existence.

The eternal perspective

As we experience more of life, it becomes abundantly clear that along with the good times comes adversity, and just as good times bring joy, adversity is accompanied by pain. There's nothing very spiritual about it. Nor does it amount to a great spiritual equation.

God, in His desire to have us choose to love Him, gave us the means to make the choice to do so. Moreover, inasmuch as we are able to choose freely in that and all other areas of our lives, we are also free to live with the consequences of those choices. Unfortunately, sometimes others are impacted more than we are.

Sometimes our choices or the choices of others bring pain.

The good news is that God is not caught off guard nor surprised when "bad" things happen to good people. Our God declares "the end from the beginning" (see Isaiah 46:10), and He knows the trials that come our way. He does not *respond* to our mistakes, misfortunes, or mishaps. He already knows exactly what it will take to lead us from our present situation to His glorious throne.

What a journey that can sometimes be. As for me, I lost the one thing that I had built my career on. I lost my ability to think and reason. I was powerless to help myself, and my pain was overwhelming. Yet, God knew, just as He knows of your situation, exactly what needed to be done.

He has plans for us, and He has put things in place to bring us to Himself, through whatever traumas and pain we have to face.

If that then is true, then the rules of life start to look different and the point of view changes. It becomes adding up the sum of all things in order to turn out a preferred outcome—meaning eternity. I don't know about you, but that gives me hope.

Just when we think that we've lost, God reveals His plan to put us back on top. We can *know* that He works *all* things together for good (see Romans 8:28) and that our living does not amount to a synopsis of all the little occurrences in our lives; it's a much greater outcome. It makes me smile knowing that one day there is an appointed end, and it's going to be worth it!

In the third chapter of Philippians, the apostle Paul writes that he wanted to "gain Christ and be found in Him" (Philippians 3:8-9, NKJV). He didn't want his own righteousness, which is from the law, "but that which is through faith in Christ, the righteousness which is from God by faith; that I may know Him and the power of His resurrection, and the fellowship of His sufferings, being conformed to His death, if, by any means, I may attain to the resurrection from the dead" (Philippians 3:9-11, NKJV).

That statement is powerful for me. It shows a clear awareness and correct understanding of life and living and eternity and the everlasting, which enables each of us to live without fear, and with strength, clarity of purpose, and joy.

Paul put it in proper perspective when he talked about all he had achieved before he met Christ. He said that all he had gained (especially religiously) was like a pile of garbage to him, compared to the excellence of knowing Christ Jesus—even when that included suffering the loss of everything that he held dear.

Six years ago, I was the operations director for one of the largest insurance companies in the country. My office was on the thirty-sixth floor of Tower One in the World Trade Center. On

September 11, 2001, I almost lost my life. It was simultaneously the worst day and the best day of my life, because it was the day I was reborn.

Michael Trinidad was a very dear friend. I loved him. He was the kind of person who could laugh and fill a room with his silliness, and it could sometimes take hours for the silliness to go away. He was the kind of person that you could almost strangle because he was such a posturing male know-it-all at times. Then, with a simple smile and a confident "I'm sorry," he'd make it all right again.

Michael died that day.

John, another friend, got out of the building but took his own life in November 2001. Delaina escaped Tower Two but was committed to a psychiatric hospital immediately after the attack and was not released from the doctor's care until 2004.

These were my friends. It took me years to stop hiding from that truth and let my Father heal me of the pain and guilt that such an immense loss caused in my life. It took me years to stop trying to fill a void and change my perspective on what happened that day and why. Faith does not require an understanding.

However, from an eternal view, if the ultimate pleasure we're following is transcendence and an eternal relationship with the almighty God, then there is grace despite the challenges.

Then finally, His grace

Jesus told a story that, if you live with it and wrestle with it for a while, you will find a deeper truth below the surface, a truth about God and life.

The story starts at harvest season in first-century Palestine.

A vineyard owner discovered that he needed more help to get in all the grapes before they spoiled. Early one morning before the workday began, he went into town looking for day laborers.

Everyone knew that day laborers didn't have full-time regular jobs, so every day they would gather in town, hoping for work. They were dependent on somebody giving them employment so that they could feed their families.

When the vineyard owner arrived in town, there were twenty-five workers waiting there. He arbitrarily picked five from those who had gathered, told them where he lived, and instructed them, "Go, put in a twelve-hour day, and I will pay you a denarius."

Three hours or more into the workday, the vineyard owner came back to the town, found that twenty workers were still waiting, and selected five more to work for him. He said, "I will pay you what is appropriate at the end of the day." He came back at noon and again at three o'clock in the afternoon. Both times, he selected five more laborers to help him. By five o'clock, just one hour before quitting time, he again returned to the town, and "to his amazement," he found five day laborers still waiting and hoping against all odds that somebody would hire them.

His first reaction was probably faithful to any human reaction. He thought that they must have still been there because they were lazy and slothful, and so he asked them, "Why are you still here?" I imagine the look on his face was probably one of bewilderment. The laborers probably returned the look before reminding him that they could not make work happen and that somebody had to give them a chance. The vineyard owner hired them as well and promised to pay them what was appropriate.

By the end of the day at six o'clock, the vineyard owner found that he had hired all twenty-five of the workers throughout the day, and all of them were lined up to be paid. When those workers who had only worked an hour came to the desk to be paid, to their amazement, they were given a whole denarius. When those hired at three o'clock in the afternoon, noon, and

*nine o'clock in the morning came, they, too, were given a whole
denarius. And then, finally, with the light of hope and great
expectation shining in their faces, last but certainly not least
came the favored five, those who had been first selected. To their
surprise, they, too, were paid only a denarius.*

*Well, when they saw what they had gotten in compari-
son to what everybody else had gotten, they were livid. They
opened their mouths and spewed venom. I imagine that these
five screamed and yelled and probably cussed, too. They did not
feel that they had been treated well, and so they demanded to
talk face-to-face with the vineyard owner. When he came out,
they said, "You have not been fair. We have worked all day long,
and some of these people have only worked an hour, and you have
paid us exactly the same."*

*At that juncture, the vineyard owner responded in a very
interesting way. He said, "Look, I have done nothing unfair. You
and I agreed at six o'clock this morning that I would pay you one
denarius, and I have lived up to my end of the bargain. Am I
not free to do with what I have as I want, or are you begrudging
me my generosity?"*[2]

When I read the end of that story, I really had to sit with it
for a while. I could see nothing fair about it. Then, the Holy Spirit
pointed me in the direction of my loved ones and friends who came
to know Jesus Christ in their dying hour. Would I begrudge them
eternal life because of the late hour? Does God not have the right
to be generous with His gifts regardless of the time? And isn't grace
more appreciated when it comes in the final hour?

I suggest to you that the question posed by the vineyard
owner is the key to our understanding. You see, there is a huge
difference between looking at life in terms of justice and looking
at life through the lens of God's grace.

We understand that indeed life is not fair, because it is rooted in grace. And if, then, grace is the root of our existence, bad things don't happen to good people—grace happens to us all.

> *Father,*
>
> *I thank You that Your grace flows down from the Cross and into our lives. Thank You for making it possible to live a purpose more profound than the sum of our victories and the gravity of our defeats. Remind us through our suffering that we have an appointed end, and that these times give us strength to endure.*
>
> *Restore in us the hope of salvation.*
>
> *Amen.*

CHAPTER 8

A DAILY DOSE OF STARTING FROM HERE

Just What the Doctor Ordered

I wanted to write something for you that was neither poetic nor biblical nor profound. I wanted this chapter to be practical and useful for both believers and nonbelievers alike. I wanted it to be useful and just what the doctor ordered.

I'd hoped that God would inspire me to something that reaches beyond a mere description of trauma, Post-Traumatic Stress Disorder disaster, or addiction and into your everyday life, knowing, of course, that He wills us to make our burdens light, He gives us the opportunity and the invitation to come to Him . . . all who carry heavy burdens. I asked if I could be a guide for you.

Holy Father,

> *Grant that in my life I may give to Your children some-*
> *thing useful from my life. Allow me to feed them and point*
> *them in the direction of Your vineyard, where they may receive*
> *food enough for life everlasting.*
> *I pray in Your Holy name, Jehovah Rapha, the Lord*
> *who heals.*
> *Amen.*

Our world today is all about the trauma. Doctors and lawyers are making a living on treating depression and anxiety disorders. New media outlets boast of high ratings as they flood our living rooms and computers with the horrors of war and terrorism around the world. Local radio and cable stations bombard us with community violence, gang raids, and drive-by shootings. Child abductions are happening right next door. We face a daily assault on our faith, and we feel unsafe mentally, spiritually, and emotionally.

> Our world today is all about the trauma. Not only are we overwhelmed by the trauma of our own lives, we're inundated by trauma from the lives of others.

Not only are we overwhelmed by the trauma of our own lives, but we're inundated by trauma from the lives of others.

No wonder road rage and domestic violence are on the rise. No wonder school shootings, office murders, and church vandalisms are out of control. No wonder Christians all over the world are experiencing apostasy and spiritual self-destruction at an alarming rate. No wonder faith as a grand theme is questioned and God's power and control are challenged.

We are medicating our children and ourselves with antidepressants, stimulants, and other medical "disasters" intended to treat trauma and attention deficit disorder, all in an effort to help us cope with the trauma.

But God gives us the ability to have peace through trauma. He has offered a way of healing those with lives broken because of drugs, alcohol, divorce, or death.

My son Eliot's favorite prayer is a very famous one. It is, "God grant me the serenity to accept the things I cannot change, courage to change the things I can, and the wisdom to know the difference." He started saying that when he was about fourteen years old, and he still says it today.

I give him a lot of credit for having wisdom beyond his years. I'm recently learning to live this prayer. I'm learning to surrender my need to understand conditions and to know that understanding is not a stipulation of serenity. Serenity comes through willingly releasing the need to know to the One who knows . . . a loving God.

Ariella, my therapist, gave me some very good advice and some strong tips on how I could use my knowledge of God to open me up to healing. She gave me a journaling exercise that started me on the road to processing the trauma. Here are the steps that I took toward being held. I hope they are both practical and useful for you in your journey.

STEP ONE:
Get out of Bed
It's difficult right now, I know, but there is a lot of sunshine out there, just waiting for you to enjoy it. Step into the light.

I boarded my windows and my doors because I was afraid the Taliban was living in the shed in my backyard. I couldn't go in basements for fear the ceiling would collapse on top of me. Getting out of bed in the morning was meaningless. There was nothing, other than the deeper recesses of insanity, waiting in my day. I suggest to you, my friends, that it's a lot easier to be who you are and to start from where you are, than it is to keep supposing that one day . . .

STEP TWO:
Find Yourself a Safe Place for Retreat
It is important that you envision a safe place in your mind that you can run away to when these exercises get to be too hard. It's hard work, but it will be worth it. Escaping to that place will help you to breathe through the pain and open you up for God's healing touch.

My safe place was my mother's living room in front of her piano as she sang. As a child when I was there, there was no place safer in the world to be. Every time I felt anxious or afraid, I immediately imagined that I was home again, in the safety of my mother's house and at her favorite spot, her piano.

STEP THREE:
Be Honest about What You Remember
It's difficult to keep all the facts in some understandable order because our mind has a tendency to skip from one thing to another. That's okay. I was told that's how we process the event. Go there. It's important not to suppress the feelings or the events.

I wrote down everything I remembered. I made special note of the smells and the sounds that I remembered. Both were particularly upsetting to me because both were so prominent in my memories of that day. It was the most terrifying thing that I have ever done. But I did it, and surprisingly, it helped.

Journaling Exercise
Write down what happened as you remember it. Write down all of the whats, whens, whys, wheres, and whos. Write down what it felt like, what it smelled like, and even what it tasted like. Write down anything and everything you can remember. Write about what you did after the event. Did you try to talk to someone or call the police? Did you run, scream, or hide, or did you pretend like nothing happened?

STEP FOUR:

Find a Soothing Sound That Helps You to Meditate

Relaxing after journaling is very important. It will help you to breathe and hear what God is saying to you about what you wrote. Play the tape, close your eyes, and just listen.

I found the sounds of the ocean and crickets very relaxing, so relaxing that on occasion, I'd sometimes fall asleep during meditation. I have to add that those were some of the best naps of my life.

STEP FIVE:

Validate the Impact That the Event/Trauma Has Had on Your Life

It's important to your healing that you don't downplay the impact that the event or trauma has had on your life and your emotions. It's a train wreck. Acknowledge it. Please, please don't hide behind God in pretense of faith. There are wounds that only you and God know about, and it's time to let Him see them so that He can repair in you what is broken, making you softer to the touch. You can trust Him.

In one of my journal entries, I wrote about how I was tired of everyone saying that I had survived for a reason. Here's what I wrote:

> *February 2002*
> *I talked to Cindy, and she told me just what everyone else has been telling me . . . maybe I survived for a reason. God has something planned for me. Doesn't He have something planned for everybody? That makes me so mad . . . arggghhh . . . who is God anyway . . . they don't even know . . . we're all probably going to die and go to hell. And so what if He does have some plan for my life . . . I'll probably just *%$#@ that up too . . . man, I hate this!!!!!! I didn't even know what day it was this morning.*
> *Dr. Rohan talked to the pharmacists today.*

Journaling Exercise
Write a list of the effects that this tragedy has had on you. Talk about the areas that you most want to hide and keep secret. Whisper them to the Lord.

STEP SIX:
Be Open and Honest with God
Trust Him with your thoughts and the full range of your emotions. This should be a "no holds barred" conversation. God has given you the right and the permission to be honest with Him. He doesn't punish us for telling the truth, even if the truth is ugly and not very Christian-like.

> Let us therefore come boldly to the throne of grace, that we may obtain mercy and find grace to help in time of need. (Hebrews 4:16, NKJV)

I noticed of lot of things about what I believed when I wrote in this area. I saw patterns of anger and doubt about who God was in relationship to the world and on a personal level. I wrote a lot about September 11 and how I didn't think my parents prepared me to face tragedy. Looking back, I realized that I needed someone to be angry with, because I wasn't honest enough to be angry with God. Seeing the truth decreased my levels of anxiety about what I should have been feeling as opposed to what I felt in reality. I think that's where our relationship started and God began to show me truth. I no longer needed to be ashamed. I felt what I felt, and He loved me anyway.

Journaling Exercise
Write out what you think of God, and then tell Him in a prayer. Read the prayer out loud, and let yourself hear the truth about what you feel. After a few days of writing in this area and reading

out loud, sit quietly for a while and experience His voice. Remember to use your tape or CD of soothing sounds (see Step Four).

STEP SEVEN:
Make God Real for You
The idea here is to acknowledge God's power and who He is. It's important to allow Him to move from the gray-haired old man in the clouds to a personal Lord, Father, and Savior. First, envision what God might look like to you. Then, identify a place in your home for you to meet Him and set a place for two. Set aside a time every day, and meet Him in the place that you set aside. Pull up a chair and read your journal to Him. The reason for doing this is to deepen your connection by making God someone more than an intangible.

This was the best and most productive exercise for me. You see, although I knew who God was, He was always my parents' God. I had never taken the time to try to make Him personal. I envisioned Him as a cross between my brother, my third-grade teacher, Mr. Broyles, and my sister, Gal.

Journaling Exercise
Write a letter to God and welcome Him into your life. Write down what it feels like to know that He is here for you. Write out what God feels like and smells like, and what it was like the first time you heard His voice. Now go back in your mind to all the times that you smelled Him and heard Him, and see Him in your life all along . . .

STEP EIGHT:
Surround Yourself with Loving, Patient Friends with Whom You Can Share Your Healing Journey
Healing is not the same as recovery. Recovery is medically defined, but healing addresses the restoration of wholeness to heart, mind, and soul. Recovery is about temporal living, and healing is about the

everlasting. This journey will be an experience that will open you up, make you vulnerable, and if you are honest, at times might be more painful than the tragedy itself. You'll need someone there for you who will always be willing to pray . . . right then . . . out loud.

I spoke most often to my brother and my pastor. They were not always happy to witness my meltdowns, but they were always there to hear them. God also gave me other friends who would not be judgmental. My friend Mimi was incredible. She slept over at times, cooked for my son and me, and watched Lifetime movies with me all night long. She went into my backyard with me, and as small as it might seem to you, she stayed out there with me and even helped me pick up leaves. All the while, she never stopped telling me, "It's okay, girl."

My friends Cindy and Melissa were incredible. They were new friends from church, and I believe they were exactly who I needed. We prayed together and talked often about Scripture and how they began their walk of faith and God's plans for my life. We even talked about their views of my life.

There are no words to express the value of their friendship during that time.

Journaling Exercise
Write about what it felt like to tell someone else about what happened to you. Talk about being honest and that person's reactions. Write about your thoughts about Christianity. Try to keep it separate from your thoughts about God.

THE FINAL STEP: SPENDING TIME ALONE . . . WITH DADDY
"Begin small and start promptly" is an old Quaker saying. The idea is to keep things simple and to begin them soon. Every great goal must be reduced to smaller intermediate goals, which I like to think of as steps.

In this journey, we take one step at a time until we reach our final destination. Getting there requires going one day at a time and having time alone with God.

I have a room in my home that I call my prayer room. It is filled with candles, fountains, and mementos that I've collected in my travels. I have books, a Bible, and even a fainting couch near the window. I go there often, and when I step into that room, I now automatically envision God there, and we start talking. I drop all the cares of this world at the door and just literally lay down at His feet.

Because I know He meets me there, sometimes I imagine that He can hardly wait for me to get a good foot into the room before He's already telling me about my day. I'm smiling back at Him as I light a candle near the waterfall that stands in the corner beneath my window. The candle creates ambiance.

As I'm lighting the candle and listening to my Beloved speak, I'm remembering that the safety He provides from this room goes beyond these four walls. It follows me into all the world, and I draw strength from that knowledge and faith from that knowledge and hope from that knowledge and trust from Him. I am remembering who I am and feeling somehow very worthy of peace and love . . . His love.

> What was once the biggest thing in my world has turned out to be just another small occurrence in relation to His greatness.

Now, as the waters fall against the small rocks in my small fountain, all of my struggles vanish beneath the small ripples flowing over the slate. I am reminded once again that it's been more than six years since my personal journey began, and what was once the biggest thing in my world has turned out to be just another small occurrence in relation to His greatness and the tranquility of time alone with Daddy in our room. . . .

The winter is past, the rain is over and gone.

The flowers appear on the earth; the time of singing has come, and the voice of the turtledove is heard in our land.

—SONG OF SOLOMON 2:11-12, NKJV

CHAPTER 9

THE GREAT OUTDOORS

Time Alone . . . with Daddy

Very early in my journey, I discovered the value of spending time in the presence of the Lord. Whether that time was in church services or alone in my home, I could sing worship songs, read my Bible, or pray for hours without realizing how much time had actually passed. I loved it.

Sometimes, I'd just be still and engage in a fantasy of conversation with the Lord that stirred me from the inside and transformed my whole self. It defined me.

Still today, I sneak away with Him, and it never gets stale

or bothersome. It's never a chore, but rather a quieting that calms my spirit and opens my soul in readiness for receiving more of His light.

So then, in the madness of my days, I break away from all the static noise and retreat to my prayer room. It's there that we meet, and being in His presence is priceless.

At this stage of your journey, I want to impress upon you the importance of tearing yourself away from the static of life, and even from recovery. I want you to understand all the benefits that you receive and give when you do that. It's important to your journey that you make time not only for God but for yourself as well, to regroup and to gather for your own healing the mind of Christ. It's stabilizing.

So how do I do that? Knowing that few words can express a meaning or idea better than the pictures, smells, and sounds of a complete story, I've penned another little tale for your interest and benefit. Bear with me here, and as you read this story, put yourself in Lil Man's shoes. Feel what he feels. See what he sees, and learn what he learns. There is a lesson here that speaks to one of the most important aspects of your journey—spending time alone with Daddy.

It was summer of 1968. I was fifteen years old, and Lil Man, my little brother, was ten years old—young enough to still be believing that daddies was invincible, but old 'nough to know better. He was a good kid. Neva gave nobody no trouble at all. 'Cept maybe when he started running 'round like a snapped chicken. But dats what he did most of da time.

Anyway, he was kinda big for his age. At ten, he was already 'bout four-and-a-half-feet tall. He had dark hair, light brown eyes, and a crooked smile that made Momma declare dat most girls would go crazy fo him when he got olda. I didn't see all dat.

He was plump, wit a pleasant round face and dimples only on da left side of his face.

Momma told him dat's where da Lord touched him first. Momma said Lil Man was the apple of God's eye, on account of he always prayed all da time 'bout every lil thang.

I think Lil Man ran 'round too much. He was always doing something and getting inta sompin equal as bad, but nobody much cared cuz boys would be boys. In fact, notes came home all da time from teachers who prayed Momma would find some way to tame the shrew in Lil Man . . . he was just plumb too happy 'bout life and outta control . . . that made most folks 'round here real tired of Lil Man real fast.

Momma didn't care. She just kep laughin' and kep 'claimin' dat no way unda God's heaven was she gonna steal 'way Lil Man's joy or kill his spirit. Dat's how Momma saw it. Dere was no way, she thought, dat she could justify stifling dat high-pitched squeal dat came from him when he was 'cited 'bout something, or dat twinkle in his rapidly blinkin' eyes when he was 'mazed, or even dat 'bunctious jump dat right thrilled her heart when it thrilled his. It was his spitfire, she said. It was just Lil Man.

Anyway, like I said, it was da summer of 1968. Lil Man was ten years old and a first time able ta go on a huntin' weekend wit Daddy. I was stayin' home. It was jes gon be Lil Man and Daddy. Da school year barely went by fast 'nough to get ta dat trip.

Finally, Saturday mornin' came. It was a gorgeous mornin'. Da wind was calm and dere weren't no 'squitoes flying 'round nowhere in sight. The air was nice and strong, and the weatha was just right.

Usually Saturday was go-to-meetin' mornings for Grandma. Daddy would go off to work, Momma would be workin' 'round da house, and Lil Man played wit his homemade army toys. He made dem out of luminum foil, and most peculiar was dat none of dose men he made had no heads. Momma told all us kids not ta tease him 'bout dat, but we couldn't hardly hold it in.

Daddy was a soldier once too.

Dat mornin', Lil Man got up wit da sun. He jumped out of bed, scampered 'cross da room and into his overalls in one fail swoop. In all da 'citement, he'd almost forgot his mornin' to dos, but he didn't. He ran right back in da bathroom, washed his face, grabbed his bristled stick to brush his teeth, and dashed for da front room. His eyes were full of 'citement, and his face was still froze in dat same grin dat Daddy had kissed on his face "goodnight" just da nite b'fo.

Daddy peeped his head from 'round da corner. "You're a lil early dis morning, Champ."

"Yes, Sa," Lil Man said. "Don't wanna be late." Daddy smiled and reminded him to dress for da tall grass and da sun.

As Daddy spoke, Lil Man's legs started twitching and his knees was moving back and forth til it looked like he jes couldn't take it no mo and he jes started jumping up 'n' down. He couldn't keep his joy spirit down. He jes fell on the floor and burst out laughin'.

"I did," he said.

By now, dere was small specs of yella light startin' to creep through da winda, and I could hear de wind movin' da trees 'round so much til it sounded like paper on da flo gettin kicked 'round. Momma was stirring 'round in da kitch'n and I could smell apple 'meal.

While Daddy packed the car, Lil Man paced up and down the yard with his bibbed cap ova his closely cut hair, his left hand in his trousers pocket, and his right holding a straw that was being obliterated by his anxious chewing.

Finally, Daddy said dose magic words, "Okay, Champ, off we go." He kissed Mom and off dey went.

Da sun was shinin' brightly by now as dey drove off into da mountains toward da wild birds. Lil Man sat quietly as Daddy hummed "Amazing Grace." Lil Man knew dat song from church.

He watched Daddy in an almost trancelike state. He wanted to be just like him when he grew up . . . and, oh boy, how much growing up it would take to be like Daddy. Daddy's arms was strong 'n' wide, and his han's looked huge gripping da steering wheel as dey drove da road. "One day I'm gonna drive just like you, Daddy."

Daddy smiled. "I know, Lil Man."

"One day I'm gonna have 'bout fifteen kids and I'm mo take 'em all huntin'. Just me and nem." Daddy smiled.

"I know, Lil Man."

"You wanna come, too, Daddy?"

"Sure, Lil Man. Maybe by den, me and yo momma might be retired. We might jes wanna watch."

Lil Man looked a little confused, but Daddy just smiled and kep driving.

Overhead, a gull flew by on what looked like big magic unflapping wings, screeching into the open wind.

"We almost dere yet?"

"We almost dere, Son."

Da drive was a bit long for a lil boy, so even wit all da 'thusiasm, Lil Man started to fall victim to da gentle breezes pushing past his face. His eyelids got heavy as da passing road signs whisked by. He shook hisself.

"Why do cars drive, Daddy?"

"You mean how?

"Yea . . . how? Who made cars, anyway?"

"You mean who invented them?"

"Yea. Is it hard to drive a car, Daddy?"

"No."

"When I grow up I'm gonna drive two cars. Can you drive two cars, Daddy?"

"Not at da same time," Daddy answered, pulling into a small area of already parked cars.

The area was broad and steep atop a mountain cliff. The ground dere was a dirt road sprinkled with covered rock, bullet shells, and ripped and dirty plaid shirts. The sound of the tires crunchin' gravel was obvious as they slowly rolled into position cliffside.

Dere was a lot of daddies dere, even some wit-out dey sons.

"Are we dere?" Lil Man asked, already unsnapping his seat buckle and scootin' up in his seat closer to da door.

"We're here. But hold up a minute, Champ. 'Memba we talked 'bout being safe out here. You stay close to me and keep dis orange jacket on ya."

Lil Man's legs was shakin' as he bounced wit 'ticipation. Slowly, carefully, Daddy unpacked his rifle and loaded bullets in his vest pockets. Next, he wrapped a whistle 'round his neck and one for Lil Man. Lil Man let out a quick giggle. Dad smiled. "Remember, blow dis if we get separated and don't stop blowing til I find ya."

"Yeppers," Lil Man responded. Somehow, as quick as a wink, his rifle was ready, his bullets was vested, his whistles was readied, and den . . . Lil Man looked at Daddy wit 'ticipation and waited.

Daddy pumped da rifle, strap't on his vest, and said, "Les go get 'em." Lil Man screamed to da top of his lungs. "Yea . . . boyee . . . les go git 'em." Lil Man wanted to clap. He felt himself come to life as he never had before. It was finally time to go and find some birds. Ahhhh, yes indeed, indeed . . . bird hunting wit Daddy; it didn't get any better than dat . . .

Da first field was not'n but tall brown grass and stalk. Dey walked hand in hand. Daddy, wit his rifle over his shoulders and his overalls pulled up cross his ches', held Lil Man's hand tightly so as not to let him 'scape into da tall grass. From wher da heavens was, I spose all God could see was Lil Man's head boppin' up 'n' down next ta Daddy's waist jacket.

Daddy and Lil Man found a spot and kneeled in da tall grass for a while, very quiet and sayin' nothin'.

"I gotta go, Daddy."

"Not now, Lil Man."

"But Daddy . . . "

Then . . . in his little voice, Daddy leaned over very slowly and whispered in Lil Man's ear. "Look up, Champ . . . here dey come. Get ready." He fixed his big old rifle ova his shoulder and braced it for Lil Man. "Now when I say pull, you pull back on dat trigger jes as hard as you can . . . kay."

Just as the birds began to fly towards them, Lil Man's mind drifted off. He looked at dose birds all together like dat. He neva sawed such a thing; poetry in movement, synchronization in position, harmony in sound and singing. It was a calming work of art. Lil Man inhaled this vision with the crisp smell of the wide open.

And den suddenly he was pulled back into the moment by the sound of Daddy's voice saying, "Ready . . . "

Lil Man quickly reached around Daddy's back and pushed da barrel of da rifle to da ground. "No, Daddy . . . please don't kill dose birds. Please, Daddy. Dey jes tryin' na get home." Tears came out of his eyes and he stared real quiet-like at Daddy . . . scared Daddy was gonna be mad at him fo makin him miss dat easy shot.

"Can we jes let 'em go, Daddy?" Lil Man asked. His voice quivered like from a winter chill. Dere was a look of pure desperation on his face. Daddy turned 'round and looked at Lil Man wit his own puzzled look. After a few seconds of

disbelief, he smiled and answered softly. "Okay, Champ, we'll let 'em fly."

Hours passed. Dey watched almost mesmerized as shades of da sun and shadows of tall grass filtered da sun's glow overhead. Together and still kneeled down in da tall grass, dey watched da wild birds disappearing into da beautiful blue sky.

Da air was still very crisp from the morning, and Lil Man believed that if he could capture at least part of the earlier morning's dew in his small hand, he could hold on to da comin' moments for da rest a his life. It was in dose moments dat Dad whispered to him all of who he was and what life would be.

Dey laughed 'bout a few things, and for da first time in his life, Daddy was Johnnie Boy. Lil Man never even knew Daddy's man name . . . he was always just Daddy. He even learned why they started calling him Lil Man.

The whistle of the wind quieted their voices from time to time, but the conversation was full speed ahead—conversation in one moment, trees bowing and swaying to the melody of it in the next. Birds held lyrics dat Lil Man was neva before acquainted with. Dey sang of the depths, breadth, and height of a father's grace in an open field beneath a broad and beautiful blue sky filled with elegance—wandering birds, gifts of surprise and delight, confidence and hope, peacefulness and purpose.

Lil Man drifted off when his eyes began to get heavier.

"Let's pack it up now, Champ. We'll stop at KFC on da way home," Daddy said.

Lil Man smiled real big, curled his lil hand up inside Daddy's hand, looked at Daddy's face, and took a mental picta of dat moment. I hear tell Lil Man said it was da best moment of his life. He said dey stayed out dere all day long, jes watchin da birds fly and talkin' and laughin' and fallin' in love wit each otha. Lil Man said it was da best huntin' trip that he neva been on . . . jes spending time wit Daddy.

Lil Man is sixteen years old taday, and he not likely to spend much time wit Daddy dese days. Mainly cuz Daddy old and Lil Man is young. Dey still go on na swing sometimes at night and talk fo hours. Momma said dat dey rise up wit da sun some mornin's.

Looking back, all dose years ago now I still member da look on Daddy's face sittin' cross da table dat nite eatin' up dat stoe-bought chicken. 'Tucky Fried still his favorite.

"Dis da best bird we ever put on dis table," Daddy said.

"And dat was da best huntin' trip I neva been on," Lil Man said.

"Jes cuz we got 'Tucky Fried?" I asked Lil Man.

Dere was a long pause 'tween eatin', and Lil Man almost looked like he want gonna answer. Den he looked at me square on, puffed up his ches' in pride, and said, "Nope, cuz I was wit my Daddy."

Lil Man smiled. I smiled. Momma smiled. Daddy jes kep a eatin'.[1]

As for me, I will see Your face in righteousness; I shall be satisfied when I awake in Your likeness. (Psalm 17:15, NKJV)

I believe it is innate to our design to seek companionship with the Lord. That our spirits cry out to Him all of our lives. That our souls yearn for His touch and that feeling of belonging.

I was blessed to know and adore my earthly father. And he felt the same way about me. We shared a connection that no one on earth could ever break, and I cherished my time with him. Dad and I would talk for hours about the Bible and boys that I liked and all kinds of things that little girls try to do to impress their fathers. Sometimes, I'd just sit upstairs in the sitting area of his bedroom with him, just watching him watch baseball. Just to be in his presence.

When he died, I held on to those memories, and they kept me near him.

I believe that God wants us to want Him in that same way. He wants us to yearn to be in His presence and spend time alone with Him, not just slated time, but also every minute of every day, actively enjoying the sweetness of Him, learning who He is, and receiving from Him who we are. He wants to have honest time with us, sharing intimate, unrestrained communion, and a place where we can make known our hearts, with all of our needs and wishes, thoughts and feelings, doubts and anxieties, sorrows and joys. He desires to hear our secrets as told by us and our hopes for everyday living, and just communion with Him.

His Word tells us to talk with Him nonstop. It says, "Rejoice always, pray without ceasing, in everything give thanks; for this is the will of God in Christ Jesus for you" (1 Thessalonians 5:16-18, NKJV). Imagine how fulfilling it would be to talk with God all the time and experience God's presence in every minute of your day. Imagine the peace, the healing, the surrender, and the joy that would come from living that way.

This is the will of our Father.

But sometimes His voice is drowned by the static noise that has become our lives, and we can get so overwhelmed by the long lists of things to do—the "round to its" and the "must haves"—that we forget to just sit and watch Him watch us. We plunge headfirst into whirlwinds of societal demands and neglect our great getaways, downtimes, and quiet moments with the Lord.

I believe that just as Lil Man's father did, our heavenly Father enjoys His time with us, whether we are fulfilling our promises,

> Imagine how fulfilling it would be to talk with God all the time and experience God's presence in every minute of our day. Imagine the peace, the healing, the surrender, and the joy that would come from living that way.

having second thoughts about the promises we made, or just being human. He delights in revealing His mind, His plans, His ways, and, yes, even His thoughts. He wants us to know Him by name, and He's provided the way.

Our heavenly Father provides a place of refuge from the storms of the world where we can cling to Him; He lends us His arms for resting our weary souls in quiet and His ears to bear our burdens. In His presence, there is recovery, healing, and rebirth.

Through spending time with his father, Lil Man discovered who he was and who his daddy really was. He approached those fields with great expectations for what he would learn about hunting. He instead got much more than what he bargained for. He learned grace, peace, and knowledge of himself. He got intimacy, forgiveness, and a deeper appreciation for life. Lil Man experienced the fullness of his father's love—the full depths, breadth, and height of it, and he was changed.

As we spend time with Him, we yearn for Him, learning more about Him, and as we learn of Him, we become more like Him. And as we become more like Him, our purpose in life is revealed. Psalm 84:1-2 says it best: "How lovely is your dwelling place, O Lord Almighty! My soul yearns, even faints, for the courts of the Lord; my heart and my flesh cry out for the living God."

I replaced my time with my earthly father with time alone with my heavenly Father, and it has radically changed the way I look at my relationship *with* God, as well as my relationship *to* God. It is now neither a duty nor a discipline. It is now neither a commitment nor a regimen that I impose on myself early mornings or late afternoons like eating vegetables and exercise. Rather, it is

> As we spend time with Him, we yearn for Him, learning more about Him, and as we learn of Him, we become more like Him. And as we become more like Him, our purpose in life is revealed.

a response to and an answer for my Father, Who has been calling me all my life. It is a relationship.

Lil Man went into the woods expecting that his time with his father would be spent hunting and doing what Daddy enjoyed doing. What he found was that Daddy simply enjoyed being with him.

> I encourage you to find time to spend with Daddy.

I encourage you to find time to spend with Daddy. Approach that time with open arms and receive grace, peace, and knowledge of yourself. Receive intimacy, forgiveness, and a deeper appreciation for life. Come closer to our heavenly Father, and experience the fullness of His love—the full depths, breadth, and height of it, and be changed.

> Stay in that secret place, till the surrounding noises begin to fade out of your heart, till a sense of God's presence has enveloped you. Listen for His inward voice till you learn to recognize it. (A. W. Tozer)

Our greatest fear is not that we are inadequate. Our greatest fear is that we are powerful beyond measure. It is our light, not our darkness that most frightens us. We ask ourselves, who am I to be brilliant, fabulous, gorgeous, talented? Actually, who are you not to be? You are a child of God. Your playing small doesn't serve the world. There's nothing enlightened about shrinking so that other people won't feel insecure around you. We were born to make manifest the glory of God that's within us. It's not just in some of us. It's in everyone. And as we let our own light shine, we automatically give other people permission to do the same. As we are liberated from our own fears, our presence automatically liberates others.

—NELSON MANDELA

CHAPTER 10

IN SEARCH OF ME

My relationship with God is the best part of me. It defines who I am. The Lord is my identity. I am because He is. If I lose touch with God, I lose touch with who I am. And so this is what I seek: to know Him more perfectly and to love Him more honestly with every breath that passes across my lips.

Six years ago I lost my identity to the stereotypes of trying to be "me" and then to the misnomers of being a September 11 survivor. I was caught between uncertainty and lies, chasing a truth that I was told could be found in my own mind.

Immediately after 9-11, I faced issues and fears that were so far outside the boundaries of my frame of reference that the psychological and spiritual issues I had to confront dizzied me. I had no idea where God was supposed to fit in all of my ideas and ideals, perhaps even my idols. My anxieties completely obliterated the possibility of any union between God and me.

Daily I tried to discover Leslie within the confines of societal definitions and the trappings of this world. I lived a superficial life of vainglory, from all the frayed edges of life's disappointments and pain rather than from the quiet center of God's promises. I had no choice but to be born again.

It's funny today. Looking back, I see so clearly now. Then, I couldn't make sense of life anymore. My thoughts were different. My sleep patterns were different. It felt like something inside me was broken, and I had no idea who I was.

> Trauma does more than steal a piece of our lives. It also steals our identity.

Trauma does more than steal a piece of our lives. It also steals our identity. It robs us of all the little things we become confident in over the years. Simple things, like a beautiful smile, become forced. A powerful voice becomes hesitant, and the strength of character that was is no more. Who are we, then, when we lose so much of who we are?

We find ourselves in constant agony, fighting against the pain all the time, battling the nervous stomachs, the sleepless nights, the emotional roller coaster, and the boomerang recovery days. Beating ourselves up about progress and regress, we celebrate the highs and sleep through the lows.

We see ourselves as weak, insecure, helpless, and lost.

I've heard a lot of opinions about Post-Traumatic Stress Disorder (PTSD) and about traumatic responses in the lives of believers. I've heard my share of misleading notions that run the full gamut of thought—from PTSD being a made-up disease with no provable basis to traumatic responses being demonic oppression. I've even heard that Christians shouldn't suffer any effects of trauma at all.

I met a woman a few years ago who showed me great compassion after hearing my witness of God's grace in my life. She asked me if she could pray for me, and of course, I said yes. As she prayed, she began attempting to cast out the spirit of fear. Afterward she told me that I should just claim my deliverance and believe God's Word. She quoted, "For God has not given us a spirit of fear, but of power and of love and of a sound mind" (2 Timothy 1:7, NKJV).

Now, I wasn't possessed with any spirit at all. I was lost in the aftermath of the most painful experience of my life and one of the most memorably horrific days in our country's history.

What I needed was encouragement; what I got was more shame. Without realizing it, she validated my feelings of unworthiness and humiliation. She confirmed that I was lost, cast aside, unloved, and of the devil. She affirmed that God had no place with me.

Consequently, my feelings of inadequacy continued to grow. My mind trained my eyes to see myself negatively. I was fat, ugly, victimized, and broken, and nothing I did would ever be good enough. I was sure that no one loved me and that my life would never get any better. I had become the tragedy.

I can't speak to this subject using the exact details or all the applicable medical terminology as I would like, but I believe that if you are a survivor of any traumatic event, words are worth about a dollar anyway. Words will not keep you from getting so easily lost in the tragedy that you survived. They won't keep you from feeling afraid and alone and from misidentifying yourself. Something inside feels so broken that your words won't keep you from believing that you might never be restored to wholeness.

At the risk of being dead-on, I'll go even further out on a

limb and suggest to you that in almost all traumatic responses and situations of severe anguish, there is an element of self-absorption that becomes self-deprecating. When you're living in a depressed state and life is spinning out of control mentally, spiritually, and emotionally, low self-esteem is inevitable. It was for me.

I felt vulnerable to the entire world and powerless against it. I was uncomfortable with life, and I didn't know which shoe would drop next or when the next bomb was going to explode. Somewhere in the darkness of my particular nightmare, I lost touch with my soul, and I had no idea where to begin my search and recovery.

> When you're living in a depressed state and life is spinning out of control mentally, spiritually, and emotionally, low self-esteem is inevitable.

Be sober, be vigilant; because your adversary the devil walks about like a roaring lion, seeking whom he may devour. Resist him, steadfast in the faith, knowing that the same sufferings are experienced by your brotherhood in the world. (1 Peter 5:8-9, NKJV)

And this, my friends, is the accomplished work of our enemy, to keep us in despair, shameful and wallowing in self-pity, thus keeping us captive to ourselves. Preoccupation with self almost guarantees estrangement from God. We cannot become obsessed with self and see God. We drift farther from God and farther from the truth. We cannot walk in self and know God. Our enemy, who is the evil one, knows this, and his aim is to keep us from our inheritance, which is the everlasting. He keeps us always unsure, unsettled, always searching, "ever learning, and never able to come into the knowledge of the truth" (2 Timothy 3:6-7, KJV) of our identity in Christ and our entitlement.

But take heart, my friends. See what love the Father has given us, that we should be called children of God (see 1 John 3:1-3);

and so we are. We are His children, and as such, we don't have to succumb to the deceit of an enemy who seeks to kill our spirits and rob us of our inheritances. The laws of trauma need not bind us. For whom the Son sets free is free indeed.

That freedom in Christ matches our characteristics to His and changes our makeup. We are now compassionate and loving. We are smart and beautiful. We are creative, humorous, and full of light. We are more than conquerors of this burden that we now give to Him. We are children of God, born to soar and live abundant lives!

> We don't have to succumb to the deceit of an enemy who seeks to kill our spirit and rob us of our inheritance. The laws of trauma need not bind us.

My heart longs to encourage you and express to you how sincere I am in seeking after your healing. I have been where you are right now. I have seen the disappointments, the ups, the downs, and the self-beatings when I saw myself as a failure in recovery.

Many who read this possibly will not understand exactly where it is that I speak from or what I speak of, but still I say to those of you who know, just walk away from it all. Do not try to know how; just give it to God and don't take it back. Dry your eyes, open the windows, shake the dust of sorrow from your feet, and walk in the light of who you are. Deny the fear. You have to believe that He is your refuge. The Lord your God is your Father, and goodness and mercy are your birthrights. They will follow you all the days of your life.

John Calvin said in his classic work *Institutes of the Christian Religion*, "It is certain that man never achieves a clear knowledge of himself unless he has first looked upon God's face."

So look to the Lord and walk now in confidence, my brothers and sisters in Christ, and in who you are. Be encouraged in your journey toward healing.

I'm not exactly sure about when we get to breathe deep again after experiencing trauma, but I do know that it's not some encapsulated moment hidden in the distant future of some far-away God promise. It is in your healing, which is your birthright. Your inheritance begins the moment you decide it's yours and start functioning in it. If you believe that you won't encounter it until some far-off day, that day will never come.

You won't wake up one morning after having decided to walk in your birthright and instantly discover you've achieved all that you're after. But you also don't want to hold the belief that your life won't begin until you get what you want. Your life began a long time ago, and the time to begin living it fully is right now.

Although this is not a journey that easily lends itself to public scrutiny, as the months pass, it gets a little easier to begin to shed the layers of the old man; the identity crisis will peel back and reveal the transformation, and you will be delighted by the person you meet in the mirror on every new day.

Finally, I suppose my grain of wisdom to offer, however small it may be, is that your trauma, in spite of its brutality and destructiveness, has delivered to you the unique opportunity, power, and authority to open yourself up to issues of profound spiritual significance and God's ultimate purpose for life. You can now know who you are, accept who you are, and receive your birthright.

As for me, I am powerful beyond my own self. I soar with the eagles in spirit. My uniqueness is my source of strength, and I walk in eternal victory. I . . . am . . . beautiful, powerful, graceful, and profound.

I *am* my Father's daughter.

Now there was a man of the Pharisees named Nicodemus, a member of the Jewish ruling council. He came to Jesus at night and said, "Rabbi, we know you are a teacher who has come from God. For no one could perform the miraculous signs you are doing if God were not with him."

In reply Jesus declared, "I tell you the truth, no one can see the kingdom of God unless he is born again."

"How can a man be born when he is old?" Nicodemus asked. "Surely he cannot enter a second time into his mother's womb to be born!"

Jesus answered, "I tell you the truth, no one can enter the kingdom of God unless he is born of water and the Spirit. Flesh gives birth to flesh, but the Spirit gives birth to spirit. (John 3:1-6)

Lord, when Thou wouldst guide me, I control myself.

When Thou wouldst be sovereign, I rule myself.

When Thou wouldst take care of me, I suffice myself.

When I should depend on Thy providing,
I supply myself.

When I should submit to Thy providence, I follow my
own will.

When I should study, love, honor, and trust Thee,
I serve myself.

I fault and correct Thy laws to suit myself.

Instead of Thee, I look to man's approval and
I am by nature an idolater.

Show me that none of these things can heal a wounded
conscience, or support a tottering frame, or uphold a
departing spirit.

Then take me to the cross and leave me there.

—A Puritan prayer

CHAPTER 11

THE PERFECT PLACE FOR ME

At the Foot of the Cross

I believe that a Christian lives in an atmosphere of prayer. A Christian speaks to the Lord with an open heart and then listens to the Lord with an open mind. Prayer is not a spiritual exercise that is performed on occasion or on command—it is a ceaseless communication between the individual and God. It's a way of life.

Of course, there is an aspect of prayer that is supplication, making our requests known to God and asking for the desire of our hearts and our needs. And, certainly, He answers. But the heart of prayer, I believe, is the preparation of our spirit to live in God as God lives in us.

Prayer does that.

It puts us in a place where we can give to God and hear His voice. It opens us up to the wonders of heaven, that we might know God.

Prayer is essential for successful Christian living, not just being Christian by association, but in being true followers of Jesus Christ and doers of the Word of God. Prayer, I believe, is the richest and most productive form of communication in the entire universe. Because unlike any other form of communication, prayer, by its very nature, actually has in it the power to change things and transform people.

> Unlike any other form of communication, prayer, by its very nature, actually has in it the power to change things and transform people.

Through prayer, we praise God and make "supplication for all the saints . . . " (Ephesians 6:18, NKJV). It is the ultimate expression of our dependence on and connection to God's will.

In the realm of spiritual warfare, which I believe is very connected to healing, it becomes evident that we need to pray for each other, often without ceasing.

I'm not exactly sure how it works, but when we pray in earnest, and that's the qualifier, the universe silences around us, strongholds are loosed, demons flee, and heaven's power meets with our authority to create life.

Jesus said, "I will give you the keys of the kingdom of heaven; whatever you bind on earth will be bound in heaven, and whatever you loose on earth will be loosed in heaven" (Matthew 16:19).

Things happen when we pray because prayer honors God and God honors prayer.

The words we lift to Him are rich, the worship is pure, the heart is honest, and everything assumes its divine order. God is reverenced when we pray—not by our words or technique, but by the acknowledgment that the act of prayer assumes. God is God above all.

It is therefore my belief that prayers are the most fruitful ground for worship, the most direct way to healing, and the purest means of devotion to God our Creator. No other words are as beautiful as those we say to God when they come from our heart—no need to dress them up. Simple. They should be accurate in representing our character and who we are. True.

I'm a writer—I suppose at least now I am—and I love words. I've been told that my style of writing is lyrical, conversational, and flowing. For me, prayer is that way. It has an underlying melody and rhythm that I imagine inspire songs in heaven. Its beauty invites notice, and its repetition allows everyone under the sound of the words to listen and hear the melody and respond in worship.

During the earlier part of my healing journey, I spent a lot of time in prayer. I loved being in God's presence and, even more, Him being in mine. You see, He consumes me, and I disappear when He is near.

I called to Him constantly and wrote to Him often about my true feelings and about the pain that was in my life. Then after reading the Psalms repeatedly, I decided one day to write my own psalm, trying of course to match the honesty and integrity of David's heart. It stirred my heart and allowed me to move on to the other aspect of the conversation—the listening.

This is my prayer—my written psalm. I hope it stirs your heart as well.

PRAYER OF RESTORATION AND HEALING

Praise You, O Lord, through this day that I am in, for You heal the brokenhearted and hear the cries of those who mourn. Baruch Atah Adonai.

Praise You, O Lord, for You have delivered me from the rising tides and the missiles of my enemy. He has sought to destroy my life, but You have increased my faith. Baruch Atah Adonai.

Praise You, O Lord, for You have ignored my words and deeds and have seen my wounded heart. My soul cries out to You! Blessed art Thou, O Lord, for You are full of mercy and full of grace.

Baruch Atah Adonai. Blessed art Thou, O Lord, for You are full of mercy and full of grace.

In my darkest hour, I look for You.

Find me, O my God, for I am lost and alone. My soul cries out to You.

Find me, O God, broken, beaten, and battered by the storms of life.

Find me hopeless, lost, and needing refuge.

Find me guilty and ashamed, and make me whole. Find me sinful and be my salvation.

For I have cursed You, then called to You and sought Your holy face.

Ha-Kaddosh, Baruch Hu—"The Holy One, Blessed be He."

No other God can hear the absence of my words and answer. None but You.

No other God is merciful and unchanging. No other God, Lord, but You, is my refuge, and my soul belongs to You. Hear my cries, O Lord, and answer me.

Where should I find You, my Father? No other God, except the God of Abraham, can heal me. Blessed art Thou, O Lord. Blessed art Thou. Baruch Haba Yeshua. Blessed is He who comes in the name of the Lord.

Should I turn to the east or to the west to see my redemption? Should I shout to the mountains or lay my face to the

ground to grasp salvation? O holy God. You, O God, alone
are mighty to give direction.
Come, mighty God, and be my strength. Come, Lord Jesus,
Restore my faith in You. Come, Holy Spirit, delight Yourself
in me and make me hope again.
I stand at the shores of life and the waters begin to rise.
With hands outstretched and facing upward
I wonder now where Jehovah Jireh hides.
Teach me Your ways, O Lord, that I will be like You.
Yeshua, You are worthy.
Create in me the faithfulness that can move Your heart.
Yeshua, You are worthy.
Teach me, Master, to love You . . . that I may know who
You are.
Yeshua, You are worthy.
Search my heart, O God of Abraham, and give ear to
my groanings.
For You are the righteousness that justifies and purifies and
sanctifies and glorifies and saves us.
And I will follow You all the days of my life.
Baruch Hashem Adonai. Blessed be the name of the Lord.
Amen. Amen.

CHAPTER 12

MIRACLES

Boiling an Ocean, Curing World Hunger,
and Saving Me

Miracles. Daniel in the lion's den; Shadrach, Meshach, and Abed-nego in the fiery furnace; Jonah in the belly of a whale; Jesus walking on water; and Moses parting the Red Sea. All miracles. By definition, they are divinely inspired supernatural protection, guidance, comfort, transformation, and healing that are suddenly available to average people.

We expect to read about them in the Bible and witness them in other peoples' lives, but never our own. We look for them to be these extraordinary moments in time or paradigm shifts that happen only occasionally and result in things suddenly going our way. What we don't expect are everyday occurrences.

We think *miracle,* and immediately we look for huge occurrences with an almost magical, unexplainable, and mysterious element, equal in greatness and enormity to boiling an ocean, curing world hunger, and saving us.

Truth is, I believe that miracles are simple and wonderful little gifts that happen to all kinds of people all the time. I suggest to you that God fills our lives with everyday little miracles designed to help us manage through the ordinary and survive the extraordinary.

> God fills our lives with everyday little miracles designed to help us manage through the ordinary and survive the extraordinary.

Although not many of us have seen the sea part in the middle to let people cross over to dry land, or been in demand to help wash the dirt from our brother's newly opened eye, we still breathe. Not many of us can speak of being vomited from the belly of a whale or of witnessing the sun standing still in the sky until our country wins the war on terror, but we can name at least one occasion when something wonderful, amazing, and unexplainable happened in the midst of our everyday.

He that has an ear to hear, let him hear.

A woman under the influence of heroin gives birth to a healthy baby boy. He is not addicted. He has ten fingers and ten toes, and he breathes perfectly.

An elderly man walks a city street. He is unkempt, dirty, and scarcely dressed. The temperature is below thirty degrees. He's wearing torn shoes, a dusty old overcoat, and gloves with holes at almost every finger. Someone stops to feed him and give him a warm blanket, five dollars, and a Bible. He has food in his stomach, a box on the corner for resting, ten fingers, and ten toes, and now he breathes.

After nineteen years of life without a father, a young man meets his father for the first time. They stand almost toe to toe, with equally wide shoulders and awkward crooked grins. Both react positively as they see on the other's face the same face they saw in the mirror that morning. A new beginning is born.

These few examples of wonderful things happening in the midst of our everyday, I believe, are most times the way God gives us miracles: quietly, subtly, behind-the-scenes, and in stories not blatantly obvious. Instead of showboating as some long-haired, white-bearded, old-man God in a robe who rescues us just before the whale swallows us completely, He delivers His miracles in ways we often take for granted.

A mother stays awake at night for four years praying for her daughter whom she last saw selling her body on a street corner to support her drug habit. One Sunday morning, the mother walks into church and sees her daughter in the first pew—clean, sober, and dressed in her Sunday finest.

A deacon is asked to help give a blessing to a man in the hospital who is not expected to live through the night. The man passes away later that night. The deacon testifies afterward that he is humbled and hugely grateful that he was where he was when he was needed. He says that he had the benefit of living out the gospel in his life.

The Bible tells us that God works in unexplained ways, moving beyond what is expected and into what is hoped for in those almost invisible things that happen and make us smile, laugh out loud, or even cry.

His desired result is always the same: that man might see God.

Miracles happen regardless of religion, race, culture, or tradition. They range from life giving to awe inspiring, and we must learn to see them as they appear.

Tess was eight years old when she heard her mom and dad talking about her little brother, Andrew. All she could understand was that he was very sick, in need of a special doctor, and they were completely out of money. They were moving to an apartment complex next month because Daddy didn't have the money for both the doctor bills and the house payment. Only a very costly surgery could save her brother now, and it was beginning to look like there was no one to loan them the money. She heard her dad tell her mom, "Only a miracle can save him now."

Tess went to her bedroom and pulled a glass jelly jar from its hiding place in the closet. She poured all the change out on the floor and counted it carefully. She counted it three times. The total had to be exactly perfect. There was no room for mistakes.

After counting, Tess carefully placed the coins back in the jar, and twisting on the cap, she slipped out the back door and made her way six blocks to the neighborhood drugstore with the huge ice cream cone that stood near the entrance door.

She walked up to the pharmacy counter and waited patiently for the pharmacist to give her some attention. She twisted her feet on the floor and made subtle noises to get his attention. No reaction. She coughed and cleared her throat with the most disgusting sound she could muster. Still, no reaction.

Finally, Tess decided to be proactive. She took a quarter from her jar and banged it on the glass counter. That did it!

"And how may I help you?" The pharmacist seemed to be a little annoyed at the eight-year-old's persistence. With a similar annoyance, but with no disrespect in her tone, Tess answered back, "Well, I want to talk to you about my brother," she said. "He's really, really, really sick, and I want to buy a miracle."

"Excuse me?" the pharmacist replied.

"I want to buy a miracle for my brother," she said. "His name is Andrew, and he has something bad growing inside of

his head, and my daddy says only a miracle can save him now. So, how much does a miracle cost?"

"We don't sell miracles here, little girl. I'm sorry, but I can't help you," the pharmacist said, softening a little.

"Listen, I have the money to pay for it. If it isn't enough, I will get the rest. Just tell me how much it costs."

Just then, a man walked up to the counter, stooped down, and asked the little girl, "What kind of a miracle does your brother need?"

"I don't know," Tess replied with her eyes welling up. "I just know he's really very sick and Mommy says he needs an operation, but my daddy can't pay for it, so I want to use my money. I want to use my money to buy the miracle."

"How much do you have?" the man asked.

"One dollar and eleven cents," Tess answered. Her small voice was even smaller and barely audible. "And it's all the money I have, but I can get some more if I need to."

"Wow," said the man. "What a coincidence." He smiled. "That's exactly what a miracle for little brothers costs." He knelt down, kissed Tess on the forehead, and told her to take him to her home. "I want to see your brother and meet your parents. I need to make sure that I have the kind of miracle that he needs."

The man who walked into the pharmacy that day was Dr. Carlton Armstrong, a prominent neurosurgeon from Chicago. He completed the operation without charge, and it wasn't long until Andrew was home again and doing well. And later, while praising God, Mom and Dad were talking about the chain of events that had led them to this and how much things had changed over such a short period of time.

Her mom said, "That surgery was a real miracle. I wonder how much it would have cost."

Tess smiled. She knew exactly how much a miracle cost . . . one dollar and eleven cents.[1]

The costs of miracles are high. They begin by approaching God with all of who you are and with great expectation, openness, and hope. It amounts to seeing, knowing, and then accepting that God cares enough in our lives to provide these sweet, tiny, or awesomely rich occurrences that give us hope. Asking and responding in anticipation—believing beyond the darkness and despite the circumstances. We hope in Him.

At one time, not so long ago, I considered myself a lost cause. I lost my job, my friends, my home, and my mind. My situation was impossible. I looked out over my life as it was. I recalled having been used, abused, betrayed, and disappointed by those who promised to love me. I was not blessed in love relationships. I'd been a victim of domestic violence, a victim of terrorism, and from my perspective, even a victim of God.

I didn't think that life had been fair to me, and even after all of the hard work and preventive measures that I'd taken over the years, I still landed headfirst into all the despair of an impossible situation. I was depressed and ready to accept a useless death with no honor or reward.

Then one night, I sat on the side of my bed in so much mental distress that I felt it physically. My then thirteen-year-old son, Eliot, came into my room holding in his mouth a tiny miracle. He looked at me, sat on the end of my bed, looked in my eyes, and asked me if I was ready. "For what?" I asked.

"Are you ready to receive Jesus Christ as your personal Savior?" he asked. "Mom, the Bible says that if you are lukewarm in your faith, the Lord will spit you out of His mouth."

I was dumbfounded.

"But I will heal him" (see Isaiah 57:14-21).

Later that night I went to the Lord. I went to Him in tears and in wanting. I went to Him in honesty and openness, with great expectancy. I told Him that I didn't love Him and that I didn't know Him, but that if He were so inclined, I'd like to start from there to be better acquainted. And, just like that, just where I was, He embraced me, and my new life in Christ and my recovery journey toward healing began. The beautiful Jesus took me by my hand and held me through the remaining dark hours of my trauma. When I cried, He held me. When I felt lost and alone, He held me, and when I felt completely hopeless and unworthy in my recovery, He reminded me of His love.

My miracle: While I was yet living in sin, I gave birth to the messenger who would deliver God's plan for my redemption. God used my only son, born outside the bonds of marriage, to lead me to Himself so I might live. He presented me with an extraordinary and undeniable miracle that brought me into a new, wonderful place in Christ and the beginning of a happily ever after.

> While I was yet living in sin, I gave birth to the messenger who would deliver God's plan for my redemption.

That's what our lives are about—arriving at that wonderful place in Christ that secures our salvation. From my perspective, that's all life is about.

So, despite what seems to be like boiling an ocean in life when it comes to seeing and experiencing everyday miracles that move us beyond the misfortunes and sorrows in life, I believe that the greatest of all God's miracles happens here and is plainly seen at the beginning of it all. The greatest miracle is simply approaching God with great expectation.

> Let us then approach the throne of grace with confidence, so that we may receive mercy and find grace to help us in our time of need. (Hebrews 4:16)

CHAPTER 13

WHEN THE BODY
CANNOT BE PRESENT

Healing Waters

"Hello?"

"Hey, are you okay?"

"I'm fine; I'm in the stairs and on my way out of the building. Where are you?"

"I'll meet you in the concourse."

"Okay."

"I love you."

"I love you, too."

It would be the last conversation I had on my cell phone that day. As I entered the concourse level of Tower One, the sounds of the crying voices rang out in the hallowed ground of the now-deserted concourse. The explosions and loud crackling of the fire were so mean that they seemed vocal and abusive. Looking around, I tried to gather all the pieces of what was left of me. There was blood on my hands.

Finally, after what seemed like hours and seconds all at once, I left the World Trade Center with no part of myself still intact. When the earth settled and finally righted itself, I left my love, my mind, and my life in the dust of downtown Manhattan.

> September 23, 2001
>
> Les,
>
> I heard about what happened and that you were in 9-11. I can't even imagine what you must be going through right now and how scared you must be. I hope you can find some peace in this somewhere. Just watching it on the news makes me cry every time I see it, and I keep reminding myself that God's will is done through all of this somehow. I hope you can remember that. God is in control and His will *will* be done.
>
> All of us have been keeping you in our thoughts and praying constantly for your recovery. I saw Eliot, and he told me you were just sleeping all the time. I also spoke with Mimi yesterday, and she told me that she would be there with you until Friday. I'm sure you're in good hands. Take care of yourself.
>
> We're praying for you.

It's remarkable to me that the word *peace* in the English Bible is the Hebrew word *shalom*. That word *shalom* refers to the absence of war and conflict and, like the word *healing*, refers to the presence of harmony, wholeness, and understanding. In other words, peace and healing are interreliant.

Without peace, there can be no healing. Without healing, there can be no peace. There exists an inescapable and obligatory interconnectedness between these two conditions.

For generations we have struggled with this concept. Our ideas about "peace" or "shalom" are not all the same. Our understanding of peace varies depending on where we stand in relation to the struggles in our lives, our perspective of

> Without peace, there can be no healing. Without healing, there can be no peace.

hope, and our beliefs in God. Whatever the positioning, we've consistently tried to gain peace through "understanding" in the absence of healing, or we've expected full recovery in the absence of peace.

Throughout the world, people are screaming for a way out of the suffering, looking for comfort and healing. As we are confronted with personal tragedies and addictions, increasing incidents of storms and torrential floods, tornadoes, terrible droughts and starvation, terrorism, and a war that no longer confines itself to a particular region, our desire for a simple peace is no longer enough.

Our souls are dying, desperately seeking rescue amid a perennial cry that reminds us of the condition of our faith. But the desire for a simple healing is not enough.

On a global scale, it is not enough to ask for one condition in the absence of the other. On a personal level, it is not enough merely to move through a recovery journey until you feel better.

I believe that inside each of us is an awareness that something is seriously wrong, and it stirs a deeper desire and longing for healing and peace. However, because of the intensity of our pain in the midst of our sufferings, even when the answer is clearly visible, it remains difficult for us to believe that we can have both.

It has been the same story throughout the years. In fact, it is told many times in the New Testament.

A storm arises while the disciples are in a boat, and Jesus is on a mountaintop praying (see Matthew 14:22-33). Matthew tells us that after Jesus made the disciples get into the boat and go on ahead of Him, "He went up on a mountainside by himself to pray" (Matthew 14:23).

Knowing Jesus as I do, I'm sure He was anticipating the storm and their reaction to it. I'm sure that He was also preparing Himself for what He needed to do. After the storm began to roll, Jesus looked down from the mountain and saw the raging waves and rain beating the small boat that His disciples were on. Calmly, He walked down the mountain through the storm, across the water, and to the disciples.

Now, let's slow down for a minute to look closer here. Can't you just see Jesus walking somewhat nonchalantly, all soaked from the rain, with a slight smile on His face? He knows that something wonderful and miraculous is about to happen.

> He does not use His authority to quiet the storm. He uses His authority to stroll through the storm.

In fact, as He's looking at His disciples in the boat, He's also looking at us. He is also walking through the storms of our lives, anticipating the result of His actions. He does not use His authority to quiet the storm. He uses His authority to stroll through the storm.

There is so much that we can glean from this story and take into our own lives that it's almost a shame to limit this subject to one chapter. So what I'd like for you to really grasp here is the power that Jesus used to call peace to Himself and keep moving through the storm.

There are times in our lives when we experience severe storms. They move through with such force that the winds alone blow us over. I put myself in the shoes of the disciples and lived their experience in relation to my life.

The rain is coming down in torrents. The boat is rocking back and forth. The disciples are afraid, confused, and sure that they are all going to drown. They wonder where Jesus is and why He isn't there with them. They try to look for Him through the heavy pounding of the water.

I'm sure their hearts start pounding when the water begins filling up their little boat at a rapid rate. They are probably panicking and frantically doing all they can to stay afloat. They are screaming at God, calling His name and trying to be heard over the noise of their own agony and the storm. I can almost see them desperately moving about the boat trying to navigate around and stay afloat. They are tired, wet, discouraged, sad, disappointed in Jesus . . . yet still struggling and using every muscle to move those oars, but almost to no avail as the wind is taking them in all directions. They have lost faith and are probably crying by now and wondering more and more about the whereabouts of Jesus.

Sound familiar?

They can't feel Him or touch Him, but they are sure that Christ knows of their struggle. This makes it even more difficult for them to understand why He has left them to suffer alone. The storm has grown beyond the bounds of human comprehension. The disciples feel abandoned. "Where did He go? Why isn't He taking care of us?"

Getting closer to the truth in your situation yet?

Oftentimes, I've found myself in situations where I've felt alone and afraid that the storm of my life was bigger than I was. I've wondered not only about the whereabouts of Jesus but about the "why abouts" as well. And then, just as I was feeling completely wiped out, I began to see His image through the torrents.

The disciples didn't see Him at first either. But as the day starts to dawn, Jesus, *knowing* their struggle, walked down from the mountain and crossed the water toward them.

The heavy drops of rain beat Him across the face and almost blinded Him. The wind blew against His back so fiercely that it took effort to keep standing. I'm sure His friends were His motivation. The waves were splashing over Him and threatening to pull Him under. In the distance, He sees the little boat being beaten. He sees the disciples struggling and calling His name. His heart goes out to them, and He sends His love ahead.

Finally, He gets to the boat where His disciples are . . . where I am . . . where you are.

They look out and see through the storm that there, upon the turbulent waters that threaten to sink their little boat, is Jesus, the Man Himself . . . walking!

Now, at this point, considering the personality of Jesus, I'm willing to bet that He had a slight grin on His face as He stood on the water next to the boat. I'm equally sure that the disciples probably thought they were dead or seeing a ghost, because in everyday life, who does that? Who walks on water and through a storm?

It was the Lord of the universe! Hallelujah! It was Jesus the Christ. The Holy One was walking on the storm-tossed seas and utterly defying gravity, science, the expectations of man, the laws of physics, and the rulers of darkness in order to deliver a clear message to those that He loved and to relieve them of their distress.

O my God, what an amazing thing! What an amazing God!

Once again, He knew that something wonderful was about to happen.

The story continues, as ours does. When all is raging around us and defeat is a certainty to our minds, the light of hope shines through when Jesus appears. When we finally see Him, we see His glory, and our desire is to be like Him. Peter attempted to step out onto the water to greet Him and sank. Jesus looked at Peter and asked one simple question to all of us watching, "Why did you doubt?"

Why did you doubt that I was with you? Why did you doubt that I would take care of you? Why did you doubt who I am? Why did you doubt that I love you and care about your well-being? Why did you doubt that I would meet all of your needs? Why did you doubt that I was bigger than the storm? Why did you doubt Me? Why, Peter, did you doubt that I would hold you up and you could be like Me?

In the midst of our storms, God may seem very remote, and we may doubt whether He knows and cares about our struggles at all. Like the disciples, we find it easy to assume the Lord's disinterest because we cannot see Him. When I consider the disciples, I realize how much I am like them. We all are. It's in our nature to see things as they appear to be and not as they really are.

It's only natural to size up the outlook by the measurement of the storm, and sometimes the storms in our lives can be so severe that no amount of effort can overcome them. All the counseling and medication and fighting and our best efforts are not sufficient to calm the winds of change. As we live, we are challenged by adversity, frustrated by our inability to overcome our problems, and found ever searching for the body of Christ, literally and figuratively. We row and we row against the wind, and we get nowhere.

I imagine that was exactly how the disciples felt. I imagine that's how you feel. But God doesn't want us to try harder; He wants us to trust Him! What is interesting to me is that Jesus doesn't just calm the storm or say, "Peace, be still." He instead says, though the storms of life are raging, "Yes, I will be with you, even unto the ends of the earth." He says, though the winds may blow, "My peace I leave with you."

My friend, the Lord is there with you, right now, wherever you are in this moment. His hands are outstretched to give you peace. However, so that you might "feel" Him more, He has placed His children in your life to be His hands of compassion and to show His love through their hospitality. Look around. I'm sure somewhere very near you are those who call you and pray for you and remind you that you are in their thoughts and their prayers.

Recently, I experienced another major storm. I'll speak more about that later. For now, the point I'm making is that during that time, I found it difficult to receive care from my friends at church. Not because I was embarrassed or prideful or ashamed. It was as simple as my knowing that God was in control and I was not afraid.

Then, as always, my brother offered words of wisdom. He told me to let the church be the church. He reminded me to let them love me and care for me. "It's as much for them as it is for you," he said.

Often, we only think in terms of receiving during our struggles, but I have come to realize that we are not alone in our storms. Many people are in the same boat, either offering to help or needing help themselves. None of us is immune to storms.

Wars, natural disasters, and diseases are reminders that the winds of change and the storms will come. All we need to do is "let the church be the church."

Jesus sees the storms we face both internally and externally, and He is the path to peace and healing through them all. As the storms rage in our lives, He is our ever-present help who brings a peace so real, so passionate, and so calming that it illuminates the fact that weathering life's storms does not lie in the greatness of our faith but in the greatness of our God!

Winding down to healing waters . . .
There is also wisdom in the journey for healing and peace. Though it is very hard won, it comes from facing the suffering and learning the profound lessons that it has to teach. The lessons are all about fearing neither suffering nor pain as we endure neither alone. We believe God for shalom.

And then He brings peace.

In 1871, tragedy struck Chicago as fire ravaged the city. When it was all over, three hundred people were dead and one hundred thousand were homeless. Horatio Gates Spafford was one of the many who tried to help the people of the city get back on their feet. A lawyer who had invested much of his money into the downtown Chicago real estate, he'd lost a great deal to the fire. He had one son and four daughters. His one son died about the same time of the fire. Still, for two years, Spafford, who was a friend of evangelist Dwight Moody, assisted the homeless, impoverished, and grief-stricken who were ruined by the fire.

After about two years of such work, Spafford and his family decided to take a vacation. They were going to England to join Moody on one of his evangelistic crusades and then travel in Europe. Horatio Spafford was delayed by some business, but he sent his family on ahead. His plan was to catch up to them on the other side of the Atlantic.

Their ship, the *Ville de Havre,* never made it. It collided with an English sailing ship, the *Loch Earn,* off Newfoundland and sank within twenty minutes. Though Horatio's wife, Anna, was able to cling to a piece of floating wreckage (one of only forty-seven survivors among hundreds), their four daughters—Maggie, Tanetta, Annie, and Bessie—were killed. Horatio received a horrible telegram from his wife, only two words long: "Saved alone."

Spafford boarded the next available ship to be near his grieving wife, and the two finally met up with Dwight Moody. "It is well," Spafford told him quietly. "The will of God be done."

Though reports vary as to exactly when he wrote this, at some time during his darkest hours of grief and despondency, Spafford wrote to God one of the most beautiful hymns we sing today, "When Peace, Like a River." Two of my favorite verses are below:

When peace, like a river, attendeth my way,
When sorrows like sea billows roll;
Whatever my lot, Thou hast taught me to say,
"It is well, it is well with my soul."

It is well with my soul,
It is well, it is well with my soul!

O Lord, haste the day when my faith shall be sight,
The clouds be rolled back as a scroll;
The trump shall resound, and the Lord shall descend,
Even so, it is well with my soul.

It is well with my soul,
It is well, it is well with my soul![1]

Finally, in light of all I've written here, the question is, Who can say what it is about life that leads us to such a peace . . . like a river? Who can say what ingredients it takes, for this person or for that person, to transform such overwhelming sadness into stillness and a quiet spirit, to bring healing, and to lead our souls to a new depth?

It is the peace of God that surpasses all understanding, a peace that we can't explain. Imagine owning real peace in the middle of a world of great darkness, in the depths of suffering, in the center of tribulation, and through the valley of the shadow of death. Imagine being steadfast and unshakable through the spiritual, mental, and physical storms of life.

Imagine peace like a river. Shalom.

Lord, my Father, as we're faced with adversity, remind us that
You are with us. Give to us, Lord, Your peace. And honor us,
Father, with Your holy and discernible presence. Help us to

see You through the storms of life and feel You bigger than the pain. Assure us that You control the seas and the winds and the storms that rage around us, and that we are safe in Your arms. No matter how chaotic and confusing things may be around us, give us Your peace, that we might know healing. Thank You, Father, for the peace of God, which flows mighty and great, like a river.

Amen. Amen.

CHAPTER 14

SO THIS IS LIFE

Falling in Love . . .

Holy Father, I pray that as I approach possibly one of the holiest nights in the history of mankind, I show all due respect. I humbly bow before You . . . face to the floor and in reverence. Allow me, O gracious and most merciful Father, to reveal my heart and the way that my mind envisions this night, without appearing to make it small. Instead, I offer my words to You as worship and an offering, that You will use them to perhaps reveal to Your children something more than just a death on a cross.

With my whole heart, I honor You.

Amen.

Years ago, *love* was synonymous with *charity*—the "greatest" of the three abiding virtues, the bond of perfection, and the way to freedom and abundant living. Love was action, faith, and the first response to human need and suffering through tragic situations and loss. Love was unfailing.

Our lives today have strayed from this fundamental premise. Our definition of *love* is now mere emotion, and what happens in the world today in the name of love is something else entirely: The lust for power, the need to "feel" intimacy, and even the desire for control. It has been reduced to our inherent need for fellowship. Translation: We don't want to be alone.

Consequently, the word *love* has become one of the most habitually misused of all words. We casually toss it about and use it to express the varying conditions of our flesh. We say we love our work and we love ice cream. We speak of loving our pets and our country, apple pie and baseball. There is the love between a man and a woman, and then finally, and most probably in the order of our perception of its importance, is the love of God.

Today, and perhaps throughout our history, the love between a man and a woman, where body meets soul, heart meets breath, is a glimpse of the truth found in "knowing" God's love and the irresistible promise of happiness through love.

Since I was a child, I loved even just the idea of love. I enjoyed seeing people holding hands in the springtime and blissfully glancing into each other's eyes. It always made me smile.

I fantasized about what my life would be like when I finally found such a sweet love. I wrote lyrical love poems and collected those "Love Is" cartoon strips, secretly placing them into a folder to wish upon. My idea was that one day the love of my life would come to rescue me. We'd sit and read those strips aloud, and then he'd glance into my eyes and see his own reflection.

I had such reason to believe because God blessed our home with love as well. I had a father who loved my mother as Christ loved the church and a mother who honored my father and was a helpmate in every sense of the word. They often kissed midsentence, were very playful together, and loved laughing out loud. In fact, sometimes at night, from somewhere upstairs in our home, my mother's laughter would suddenly penetrate the darkness of the night and remind us that Daddy was funny—not a trait that we often saw.

My mother didn't stop smiling at my daddy until she died.

In that perfect picture they painted for me, I believed that one day I would grow up and experience that very same thing in my own life.

As I got older and began to date, life happened to me. The pretty picture of love withered under the harsh lights of physical and sexual abuse. Each relationship began with a promise that this one would be better than the one before, and each one ended with the revelation that they were all the same. Eventually, I lost hope of finding a man like dear old Dad and owning my place in a marriage as my mother had. I became callous and distant, and the lack of a true love of my life became my secret bitterness and the fear of my own heart. I decided not to want it.

I believe that it's that simple for many of us. We hold onto an interesting concept that love is beyond us, that it comes like the wind, taking us by surprise and stealing our breath away. Our buy-in is that love is a life force between man and woman that is neither premeditated nor self-willed. We believe we fall into love, that it imposes itself upon us, bringing with it the unique and unequaled power to determine the greater part of our happiness. Our rationale is that anything with such strength that comes by itself can also leave of itself. While this is indeed a natural truth, love does not adhere to this rule. Love is supernatural.

So then, having no real clue of what love is all about, we deny ourselves the joy and excitement of wanting love because of the fear of not having it. At least, that was true for me. I found it just easier to grow increasingly bitter and hide behind old wounds that would never heal without the very thing I was hiding from, Love.

> An interesting thing happened on my journey to healing. I met a Man.

And then one day, an interesting thing happened on my journey to healing. I met a Man.

In many ways, I believe that my journey might be similar to yours, which might be similar to Peter's story. Follow me as I follow Christ.

We walked all day until finally we came to rest in a beautiful, old, walled garden in Jerusalem, east of the Mount of Olives, called Gethsemane.

It was dark that night, but the stars cast a very intimate glow across the skies. An unusual evening—mist floated in the air and lingered there for hours. Crickets did what crickets do, but only longer. The grass, still a little dry from desert winds of the day, drank deeply of the mist as it gave place for Him to kneel.

There were eleven of us. We sat quietly for a moment, listening to the tickling of gentle winds moving between small bushes around us. Small conversations started but quickly moved to silence when He moved away to pray. "Stay awake. Watch!" Love said to us as He removed His shawl and walked away to pray.

Usually we prayed together, standing, with our eyes open and lifted to heaven. This night, I saw Him more serene and urgent as He spoke to God.

The others drifted off quickly. I lingered for a while and watched Love as He spent time alone with His Father. Still unsure of my place in the family and learning to cry "Abba, Father," I mouthed the words in hesitation each time that He did.

The warm glow from the moon falling through the trees fell near the rock where He knelt. It was trancelike. I couldn't help but drift off to sleep.

Jesus prayed. "Father, if You are willing to do so, remove this destiny from me. Even so, I want what You want." An angel from heaven appeared to Him and strengthened Him. Being in distress, He prayed more earnestly, and His sweat was like drops of blood falling to the ground.

The grass drank deeply of each drop. The essence of Him that created it could do nothing less than make it richer beneath the place where it fell.

"Father, if it is possible," He said. But we know that all things are possible with God. His mind went back to the beginning. Where in the beginning was the Word and the Word was with God. He was the Word. In the beginning, where together They decided to mold Their love into Their likeness and call Him man. Love was there.

Now, this night, for the first time in existence, Love was contemplating the inevitable separation of Himself from Himself for the love that He created.

Our relative minds cannot possibly grasp the full enormity of what this means. The visual for what actually took place is unfathomable. Spiritual things are spiritually discerned.

But there, in that garden so beautiful and rich, He felt what it would be like on that next day when He'd take unto Himself all the sins of the world and be changed from the Holiest of Holy into the one thing His Father hated the most . . . sin. For how could He take on all sin without becoming sin?

What, then, of His blessed communion with His Father? What of sweet fellowship and tender moments and purity? How can that relationship continue while He was fatally contaminated with sin and shame and more sin and inestimable sins of billions and trillions and even zillions of humans who then inhabited and who would inhabit the earth? There is no fellowship with sin.

> *Jesus prayed, "Father, if You are willing to do so, remove this destiny from me. Even so, I want what You want."*
>
> *The sun rises. The heat is intense. It was not what we expected. It was not what anyone expected. The smell of dirt and desert dust, mingled with the heat and sweat of hundreds of bystanders, the odor of blood and drear death—a commonplace scene for public games and crucifixions, but hardly the sights and smells and fragrance of Love.*

Yet, amidst the horror of Love defeated, beaten, broken, weakened, and humiliated, Love reigned. He gathered to Himself all the strength He could muster, lifted His head, and reigned supreme. His first decree must have seemed as ridiculous then as it does now. "Father, forgive them, for they do not know what they are doing."

> Many waters cannot quench love, neither can the floods drown it. (Song of Solomon 8:7, KJV)

With all that in mind, and just as an aside, it's important to note that an incredible amount of energy is released in the form of heat and gamma radiation when a single atom splits. The process of splitting happens very quickly, in approximately a picosecond. (A picosecond is one-trillionth of a second.)

The two atoms that result from the fission later release beta radiation and gamma radiation of their own, as well. Critical mass happens. And so it did. The skies grew dark, and thunder rolled. The mountains split from the earth, and heaven threatened to fall from the skies. For less than a split second, but for what must have felt to Love like forever, God the Father and Creator divided

Himself, became sin in one half, and in the other, turned His face to the repulsive sin that hung on that cross.

The pain of the cross was not the agony of being tortured by whips and ridiculed by words. It was not the raggedy, splintered old cross He carried, or the crown that pressed against His brow or the nails that went through His hands and feet. It wasn't the sword that pierced His side that He agonized over the night before. It was the price of becoming sinful man . . . separation from God.

What once was His glory had become His enemy—for His love, for His passion, for His creation . . . for me.

Then Love proclaimed, "It is finished," hung His head, and died.

Finally, when the dust clears, sunset comes, we see Love returned to the Father's right hand and in fellowship with the saints, and we find, clearly, that love truly does conquer all.

I know Love, and I call Him Jesus.

> I know Love, and I call Him Jesus.

For God so loved the world that He gave His only begotten Son, that whoever believes in Him should not perish but have everlasting life. (John 3:16, NKJV)

Life can deal us some crushing blows at times. We can suffer through the upset of trauma and pain and guilt associated with all kinds of stuff in our lives that causes us to feel like love doesn't exist. We look for it in our family and friends, but even as they surely do love us, there is no greater love than what has been shown to us by Jesus.

So then, just before we have our very own garden party, we come to the table pondering our journeys . . . without all of the answers. We come in to dine with Him, just as we are—all confused, broken, battered, worn, and upset—and we lay down all of who we are and what we have before Him. We sit with Him in the middle of all of the miracles of how and reasons why . . . the questions we can't answer and the ones we want to ask.

We come in with all the heartache and disappointments, the pain and heartbreak, the sadness and death, and for one beautiful second, we glance into the eyes of Love while dipping our bread. We come in with our addictions and convictions and terrorist attacks, and we inhale the true meaning of life as we drink a bit from the cup of faith, and we *know* then . . . it has been worth it all, proving, at last, that Love really does conquer all.

This love alone has the power to heal and transform, making our huge problems pale beneath the light of the Son. This love offers solace and refuge from the storms of life, and there is something so beautiful about finding and falling in love—especially when you *know* that that love will never hurt you, lie to you, betray you, beat you, or leave you. It's liberating.

I know that love. I call Him Jesus.

Like you, I have lived in the upset of trauma and been in situations where I didn't just think people didn't understand; I knew that they didn't get it. How could they possibly understand the gravity of what was wrenched from my dying hands? I know too well the stench of a not-so-good prognosis of recovery.

However, Love goes beyond that, and this is life. Emerging from our darkness sometimes requires a darkest night of the soul, or as my son, Eliot, describes it, a life-changing event.

Love's story in the garden of Gethsemane is that darkest night—the intrinsic connection between suffering and transformation and the necessity, in that process, of being willing to carry tension, disappointment, and unfairness without giving into despair, bitterness, blame, and the urge to just give up.

I know Love. I call Him Jesus, and I gladly follow His example through my hard times and into my own gardens. Although the results are not as universally humanity altering, I gladly surrender myself to whatever life brings my way in order that I might remain in Love and He remain in me. With so sweet an outcome, wouldn't you? I guess the better question is . . . will you?

Let's pray once more.

Again, breathe life into us, Father, that we might live always in Your presence. Help us to daily remember the real price Love paid that we might live. Grant that in praise and thanksgiving, we may offer ourselves to You and receive Your perfect Love. Change our hearts, dear God, that we should be like Love.

Amen.

CHAPTER 15

. . . AND BEING HELD

At one time in my life, I knew an anguish that was so powerful
that I could actually hear it stirring inside of me. . . . A tear slipped
down my face and I began to write. . . .

> *Journal Entry—1/23/02*
> *I woke up on the bathroom floor again.*

This chapter has been rewritten from its original content.
Originally, it was a beautiful story about the birth of my only son,
Eliot. I wrote about what it was like being a single mom and being

captivated by tiny little hands with amazing grip. I wrote about his sense of humor and holding him through his childhood pains, nightmares, and ear infections. I even wrote about how difficult it was for me to watch him grow from being totally Mommy dependent to being his own man.

Then in August of 2006, the universe collapsed when I drove my baby boy to college and left him there. I had no idea how the sun would shine if his eyes didn't inspire it.

But as much as it pains me to let him live his own calling, it pleases me to see him walking in his anointing and growing up to be a man of God. He has a holy boldness with regard to the things of God, his passion for God, and his love for God's people. The wisdom that God has given him is beyond his years. Eliot is an amazing young man, and I'm so blessed to be his mother.

And that was the chapter—all about love and being held. Then just as I ended it with what I was sure would be a brilliant and catchy little phrase, saved the file, and prepared to hand in this work of art to my editor, the Holy Spirit changed the script. Isn't that just like Him?

I was left thinking, *Now what?*

"Now what" is that recently my life changed again. I was living with all intent for Jesus Christ and enjoying the even flow of my everyday when life knocked the wind out of me . . . again. Once again I found myself on my knees and struggling to breathe.

So now in living this new awakening, I am compelled by Him who restored my breath to share a renewed hope with you.

Although it's my story being told, the background narrative is written from three parallel points of view: my mother's (telling of my birth); mine (telling of Eliot's birth); and our heavenly Father's (telling of our birth). I believe this to be everyone's story.

It sings of hope and faith, love, mercy, and the peace of God that comes only with being held.

It begins.

I was born and raised in a very religious home in Chicago. As a child, I was sickly and very fragile. Most of my time, as I recall, was spent with my brothers and sisters.

> *My beautiful child,*
>
> *I remember the day that you were born. You were the most beautiful little creature that I'd ever laid my eyes on. You smelled of . . . new. I was pleased with myself that I'd made a little me, and I struggled to keep myself from just drifting off into the sheer delight of what my love had made.*
>
> *I basked in your beauty. Your skin was soft like paper and warm to the touch. Your tiny fingers thrilled me, and all I could do to keep from crying tears of joy every time I laid eyes on you was to hold you . . . adore you. Cheek to cheek, I lifted your tiny face next to mine and smothered you with big, warm kisses.*
>
> *New life smells better than Christmas toys.*
>
> *All eyes were on you that day . . . except for yours. Yours followed me, focused on mine, and smiled. Your tiny hands reached for me, and though no one else even knew that I was there, you gazed at me so adoringly.*
>
> *You were so tiny, so helpless, and so . . . perfect. Your little hands were soft and longing to touch. Though no one else paid attention to me, your little eyes followed me everywhere. You stole my heart. I remember that moment like it was yesterday.*
>
> *The milky smell of your breath embraced me as I held you to my bosom, watching your eyes close slowly from peace and contentment. Did you know that you were as safe then as you ever would be . . . in my arms? This I promise you, that if you let me, I will always hold you close to me.*
>
> *You fell asleep with your fingers in your mouth and that strangely personal smile on your face.*
>
> *That's when I first missed you. It's funny to remember*

now just how much I missed you, even when you only slept. I examined every inch of you—I counted every finger, every toe, and every strand of hair.

My mother was a whirlwind of a woman. She was strong in everything she did. She walked through life as if her purpose were to make it happen, and in most things, she did. She loved really hard and lived even harder. Her legacy to her children, called faith, was a driving force of hers.

As a teenager, I got stronger physically and mentally. My mission in life was to drive my mother to drink or to drive her crazy . . . whichever came first. Neither happened. Instead, as my will got stronger, so did her faith. If Mom said jump, I sat down. If she said sit down, I ran kicking and screaming from the room. All the while, although she did not "spare the rod," she kept praying and telling me that one day God was going to do mighty things in my life. I had no idea at the time, but those prayers would follow me all the days of my life and help to deliver me from falling towers beyond my control.

One day you'll know this feeling. It's what makes a parent. This intensity—this something from the universe that wrenches at the heart until there's nothing left to it but . . . connectedness and belonging. It's how I came to be yours and you became mine. It cannot be seen or touched, and yet it's such an integral part of the parenting experience that it penetrates the very soul. I laugh at myself . . . how I came to create such a thing . . . so perfect.

I loved watching you sleep. Let me tell you a secret, my darling.

It's been a joy, these years that you have given me. It's been my gift to watch you run and play, to see you off to school each day, to be there for you when you came in from school, struggling through kindergarten and phonics and sixth grade and Mrs.

Verge and politics. You've thrilled my soul by inviting me into your room at night to hear your stories of first friends, firstfruits, and first . . . everything. I've smiled through your tantrums and demands for chocolate chip cookies for dinner and juice at three o'clock in the morning.

I remember the house filled with your kindergarten songs of Mr. Sun just as clearly as if it were your high school homecoming chants of victory . . . or was it defeat?

Eventually, I had enough of the pious living taught in my parents' home. I wanted power, prestige, and corporate success. What I didn't want was my mother's faith or her God. My mother passed on January 1, 1982, and I left Chicago in hot pursuit of corporate dreams and independence. I found them both. In 2001, I became one of only two black operations executives for one of the largest insurance companies in the country.

My offices were on the thirty-sixth and thirty-seventh floors of Tower One of the World Trade Center. My personal space boasted floor-to-ceiling windows with breathtaking views of the city.

I'd arrived. I'd arrived at twelve- to fourteen-hour workdays, corporate power lunches, and all the glamour of New York City. I used my title and position to gather as much expensive "stuff" as my home and pockets could hold. I lived in the best community, sent my son to the most expensive prep schools, and worshipped all the things that my hands had made. There was no need in my life for God. I was god in my life, and nothing was going to change that.

Did you know that I've saved every memory that you hold dear—your first Christmas, your first date, your first car, the first time you fell in love? I even saved your first heartbreak. I collected your tears.

It's poetic, don't you think—my holding you again through

heartbreak? It is bittersweet for me. I said aloud that I would never let anyone or anything hurt you, not even you . . . nothing hurts me as much as losing you to your own pain; and nothing moves my heart like comforting you. I love you.

Ever watched a bird fly? The sheer beauty of its flight, soaring through the sky with such a marvelous ease and perfected blending of harmony and freedom. It takes off, flies with twists and turns, soars and dives, and lands again on a tiny branch, all with effortless precision. That's how I love you—with effortless precision and a freedom that soars. . . .

Then in an instant, my life was over. One September morning, someone dropped a plane out of a beautiful blue sky.

Wake from your sleep, my darling; I see you drowning in your tears. It breaks my heart to watch you hurt.

On September 11, 2001, I got up out of my antique cannonball bed, dressed in my designer finest, grabbed my laptop, and went to war. From the moment of impact, my brain went numb. When the first plane hit, I was standing in front of one of those floor-to-ceiling windows, feeling the building sway back and forth and watching huge pieces of furniture and paper and body parts fall outside. They banged the side of the building.

I stood mesmerized for a few minutes and watched the bodies fall. My mind took me nowhere.

My eyes followed you through your day that day, and when that thing happened and your knees buckled, mine did too. I recall watching intently, too intently, your struggling heart and every weary breath you fought to breathe, almost forgetting to inhale. Your existence was the center of mine.

I heard you call for me, and it shattered me to hear you

that way. The sound of your voice . . . my hands trembled. They wanted to reach for you. My instinct was to grab you up and take you far from that . . . place . . . that . . . thing; but I couldn't.

Remember, I promised I wouldn't interfere, that I'd let you live your life.

I lost twenty-two of my friends and a man that I loved. Eventually, I lost my mind and was diagnosed with Post-Traumatic Stress Disorder, and because I wasn't mentally functional, I lost my career and my life savings.

Eliot and I became homeless.

Over the years, I was so emotionally wounded, so spiritually distressed, and so raw that I thought I would never heal. I didn't think that I would ever be able to stop being angry and supposing that every plane crash, every fire was a terrorist attack.

Your instinct was to search for—and expect me to put in front of you—a great big divine firewall to shield you from that thing you were so afraid of . . . there really are no such things as monsters, my darling. But was I supposed to shield you, even though I promised that I wouldn't?

You screamed when it didn't come. You shook your little fists at heaven and rebuked all of divinity in one single gesture, and one tiny but massive tear that fell . . . from me . . . covered you.

Eventually God delivered me a miracle from the mouth of my son, Eliot, and I gave my whole self to Him. I realized that this journey with Him would be a forever one, and I enjoyed living it. I've learned through the upset of September 11 not to take life for granted, because it's fleeting. So, just as my mother did, I live hard and love harder, one day at a time and one step at a time.

Recently, God has been talking to me in the matter of

surrendering my whole life to Him, including my marital status. I pretended for a while not to know what He was talking about. I was busy being in ministry and being mindful of the things of God.

I founded a nonprofit to help the homeless and victims of domestic violence. I fed the homeless on the street and worked tirelessly in every ministry opportunity that I could. I led the singles ministry at my church, and I even declared myself an evangelist.

Then one day I was reminded of a phrase I'd heard: "Nevertheless, I want what you want."

When you woke from your sleeping, I greeted you with "Good morning, Bright Eyes. Got a smile for me?" You always laughed, and your smile lit up my life. All I want is what's best for you . . . all I will ever want is what's best for you.

It had been more than five years since I was romantically involved or even interested in anyone. I had no idea how to date, how to talk to a man about anything other than God, or even how to laugh at cornball jokes. What if I met someone and I didn't like him? And even worse than that, what if I met someone who didn't like me? *Are You sure about this, God?* I was scared to death.

Still, I hopped back into the dating game. I started working out again. I let my hair grow, colored it, and even combed it. It wasn't long until I had dropped the eighteen pounds that I'd spent five years collecting. In no time at all, I was looking at eligible Christian men, and they were looking at me. It was kind of fun, seeing the awkwardness from both of us. At my age, you'd think I'd know how to "just get on with it."

Well, I met someone. He was great. He was funny, smart, full of good ideas, and he had a passion for the homeless and a love for the Lord that matched my own. We prayed together and talked on the phone for hours into the night. Secretly, I started calling him "husband" and imagining a whirlwind of changes to my pink, flowered master bathroom décor.

It was Wednesday night. I was on my way to prayer meeting at the church. The plan was to attend the prayer service, and then I'd meet my friend afterward for a cup of coffee and a chat. I showered, and as I dressed in a good-looking, but not-so-obvious jean outfit, I noticed a lump in my right breast. It was like a gut punch that knocked the wind out of me.

I looked in the mirror, examined it, and found that it was a little larger than the size of a large walnut.

Thump! That was the sound of my heart falling from my chest to the floor. My hand grabbed my stomach, and I struggled for air . . . *Breathe, Leslie.* That was familiar. I inhaled, then slowly exhaled, and then I inhaled again . . .

God, what are you doing? How is this supposed to work? You change my heart or open it up to dating, and then you threaten me with cancer? What good can come from my demise? Where are you? What have I done to warrant this?

> *I remember you, my sweet baby, on a night that doesn't seem so long ago. I sat by your side as you wept. I cried with you; to see your pain is to know pain intimately. I watched you cry and hold your head between your hands. You cried until you fell asleep.*
>
> *I placed my hand on yours and whispered sweet nothings in your ear as you slept. Remember how you thought it was odd for such a quiet wind on a late autumn night? Your eyes flickered underneath their lids and I kissed your brow . . . my little one . . . how I love you so. . . .*

I told myself not to panic. It can't be cancer; life can't be this cruel . . . can't be this imbalanced. I sat on the side of my bed and cried until my head hurt.

I kept thinking about Eliot. *What would happen to him now? What would he do without his mother? He won't be able to handle something of this magnitude . . . not again.*

We were just getting back to life, and now here we were again being forced to face my demise. I thought about all the things I'd done over the past few years and how much more there was for me to do . . . at least by estimations.

Then, in a subtle wind of change, I got answers.

The LORD himself goes before you and will be with you; he will never leave you nor forsake you. Do not be afraid; do not be discouraged. (Deuteronomy 31:8)

Be strong and courageous. Do not be afraid or terrified because of them, for the LORD your God goes with you; he will never leave you nor forsake you. (Deuteronomy 31:6)

The peace of God came over me. I was okay. My prayer changed direction. Instead of asking for healing, which I know is mine either here or in the everlasting, I asked God to give me His peace and show me how to be faithful to His will. *Shalom.*

I would not go kicking and screaming. *Shalom.*

I choose not to be a victim of cancer or anything else, but to live victoriously until the everlasting. *Baruch Hashem Adonai.*

I was not afraid of heaven . . . of seeing God. Life couldn't threaten me with the very thing that I live for. *Shalom.*

Once again, the peace of God covered me. I relearned of His grace, and I was amazed at how His simple words brought so much peace, comfort, and direction. His words guided me and gave me hope to endure at least one more derailment. . . .

The very next week, while everyone around me showed appreciated concern, things happened fast. I was in the doctor's office having a mammography, ultrasound, and then a needle biopsy. I sat with the doctor, who suggested the best course of action would be a lumpectomy. We scheduled the surgery that day.

I remember the first time you slept in your own bed. You were so proud of yourself the next morning. I missed you all night, and the truth is, I wanted to keep you a child for the rest of your life. Then I'd know that you'd never love anyone else but me. Instead, I let you grow.

Looking back, as much as I hate to admit it, for a split second or more in the beginning of this particular event in my life, I was consumed with fear and angry with God about the course my life had taken. One minute I was back in the saddle dating, and the next, I was feeling less than whole, ugly, unattractive, and destined to want for something that I would never have. In what amounts to about five minutes of emotional turmoil and humanity, vanity was all I had. I wanted to feel pretty again, to have some wonderful and handsome man look at me and see his own reflection. I forgot about Love, and I wanted to be in love again. There I was facing my mortality . . . again. It wasn't the idea of death that bothered me; it was the fact that once again, life and trauma were happening to me and . . . and I was being forced to respond to it . . . without warning or preparation.

I don't know, perhaps it takes a lifetime to adjust to living in a vessel that hates change in a world that thrives on it. Whether we survive our own traumas in the form of hurricanes, terror, or illness, or whether we experience someone else's alongside them, our vessels are not equipped to carry us.

> Perhaps it takes a lifetime to adjust to living in a vessel that hates change in a world that thrives on it.

Maybe that's what upsets all of us. We know that we can never trust in the security of life. It has its ups and its downs, and there isn't the death of later and the life of now. There is only the potential ending of every moment. It makes every moment full of risk. It also enriches each interaction, each instant, and each good-bye.

Then again, maybe that's the lesson here. Life is easily broken, and every moment therein has the potential to lead us into a gut punch that steals our breath away. It takes faith to really embrace this life and let go of our resistance to it. Through our upsets in life, God gives us meaning, not answers. We should take those meanings and use them to live in the knowledge of who we are in Jesus Christ—people with stories that are designed to reveal God's glory in some way—then trust that He has beautifully equipped us to live that story's purpose . . . not its outcome. That is faith.

The surgery was December 4, 2006. My pastor's wife, my good friend Shannon Torres, was with me. She prayed, and Lynora, my other friend, called constantly, and Adrianne stopped by to make sure I wasn't hanging curtains (that's another story), and my family prayed for me. My sister LaVerne was an incredible strength.

> *My darling child, as you're reading this letter, I hope that life finds you well. I hope that through all the conditions and circumstances you've lived, you've learned of my commitment to you as a parent and a friend. I want nothing more. As you continue your journey of life in the absence of my face, know that I am always with you. Know that you are loved. And although you might at times doubt that I am keeping you from harm, never doubt that I am keeping you and that you are being held.*

The surgeon removed the entire tumor and sent it to the pathologist for biopsy. I'm awaiting the results. You should know, my friends, that whatever the outcome, it already is what it was intended to be. Either way, whatever happens next, God has already sent a million tiny little miracles my way, and I am confident and strong because I know He keeps me from harm. I am comfortable and hopeful because I know that He loves me. I am peaceful and surrendered because I know that I am being held.

Update: Today is Friday, January 5, 2007. The tumor was benign. I am cancer free!

Humanly speaking, it is possible to understand the Sermon on the Mount in a thousand different ways. But Jesus knows only one possibility: simple surrender and obedience—not interpreting or applying it, but doing and obeying it. That is the only way to hear his words. He does not mean for us to discuss it as an ideal. He really means for us to get on with it.

—Dietrich Bonhoeffer

CHAPTER 16

AND NOW, SURRENDER
Perfect Submission, Perfect Delights

I was taught to ask God for what I needed, believing that He would give me whatever I asked for in His name.

So, I asked God for prosperity, power, popularity, success, health, and wealth. In all these things, I asked God for more of what I wanted, but He gave me more of what I needed. He gave me Himself.

I am, therefore, now on a mission to deliberately increase the bonds of our relationship, and in doing so, to give completely every ounce of who I am to the Lord—to stand before Him naked, after having peeled back the layers of my burdens and given all. I surrender all my doubts, the ones that I call uncertainties. I surrender my hopes, the ones that I'm afraid to say out loud; and my fears, the shy and nameless ones that have so easily beset me for so long and dulled my pleasure, clouding my joy with misery and apprehension. Gradually, I'm chipping away all of the false ideas and wrong concepts that limit my perception, and I'm living surrendered, finally experiencing life.

I believe we should all seek after that.

These are hard times today. People are struggling. Sons and daughters are off at war, families are falling apart, finances are uncertain, employment opportunities are fewer, and things just seem to keep going further and further downhill. In fact, the closer we get to what we view as the bottom, it seems the faster we fall and the more out of control our lives become. It's no wonder that our first reaction is that of feeling helpless, lost, and alone.

Tragedy throws our lives out of balance. This world has convinced us that when hard times come, it must be because we've done something wrong. There are moments of such desperation that we can feel so battered and beaten and discouraged that we wonder where God is.

As believers, we petition God and try bargaining with Him to restore to us a control that we never had to begin with. As human beings, our tendency is to re-create the place where the trauma happened or reinvent the relationship that let us down, in hopes of changing the outcome.

I believe that on some odd, subconscious level, our attempt to dredge up our original wounds and regain admittance to the place we believed was our authentic place of security—where we lived before the storm came through—is nothing more than attempts to control the journey.

For some of us, our entire lives have been never-ending journeys to recover from one something or another.

It's no wonder that we feel lost and alone. No wonder He is to us only a concept of holiness . . . not a spirit that we can touch or be touched by. We strain our brains to "get it," and still somehow we miss it because we have yet to really . . . I mean really . . . feel Him.

It's no wonder that we envision God not as a "good Father" but as some mystical, faraway, deadbeat dad standing off in the distance, just watching our lives happen. We want a real God to stand with us when job-loss storms suddenly come and blow through our lives like a whirlwind. We want a real God when cancer and other diseases strike our hearts like lightning. We need a real God to fight with us when terror attacks and earthquakes and personal loss explode in our lives like thunder. We want and need a real God to reassure us through our fears, when we risk vulnerability, seeking love, healing, and wholeness.

We want to know Him and feel Him through the storms of life and *know* that He is really there. But our faith has been shaken. Our hearts have been broken so many times that it is hard to trust . . . even God . . . even our Father. Our tendency is to believe that either we have shelter or we have the storm. We have comfort or we have pain.

But that's not biblical.

The Bible tells us we have both. It assures us in 1 Corinthians 15:57 that we are victorious through Jesus Christ. His Word declares that our Father, who is God, holds us through the pain of our lives, gives us victory, and provides rest through the storm.

> Our tendency is to believe that either we have shelter or we have the storm. We have comfort or we have pain. But the Bible tells us we have both.

The psalmist in Psalm 27:5 said, "In the day of trouble he will keep me safe in his dwelling; he will hide me in the shelter of his tabernacle and set me high upon a rock." In Psalm 32:7, David testified, "You are my hiding place; you will protect me from trouble and surround me with songs of deliverance." Psalm 62:5 shouts it loudest and probably best. It says, "Find rest, O my soul, in God alone; my hope comes from him."

Jesus Christ is our hope. He is our shelter. He is our resting place, and He is a *very real God* and *Father* . . . waiting for us to abandon ourselves, believe that He cares, and trust in Him completely.

He's waiting for us to surrender.

Surrender—not the surrender that points to giving up and not fighting anymore. That's little more than compliance. What I mean little by surrender is the verb that requires action. I mean complete acceptance of what *is* and then an intentional release of that *is* from your hands and control, into God's hands and control.

That is the longest mile, I know. I'm on that road myself. But I'm not walking alone, and I'm not afraid anymore. I'm not afraid to hope in Him. I'm not afraid to love Him. I'm not afraid to *not* know what the future holds for me, and more importantly, I'm not afraid to let go of the pain in my life.

I now know that letting go of the pain and doubt that restricts access to healing is the hardest part of that healing. It's a very long road to travel, but you can get there from here! Just let go. Let yourself believe that God is mightier than the storms in your life. Believe that He is God and beside Him, there are no equals.

Gladly, I'm closing my eyes, stretching out my arms, and falling . . . into the waiting hands of my Father's rest.

Our Father wants us to abandon ourselves to Him. He wants us to hope in Him by letting go. Oh boy, that's a mouthful, isn't it?

It's difficult to just "hand over" control of your life to someone you can't see. We want to be able to see it, touch it, and feel it before we believe it. Even in our most trying times, we want to see God before we can believe that He's there.

I heard a story once about a deacon. For the sake of making the story more personal, we'll call him Deacon Jones. Well, Deacon Jones lived in the Catskill Mountains of New York state, and he loved driving through the mountains on the weekends.

Every Friday, he'd drive up to the mountain and camp out until Saturday afternoon. He'd make his hour drive and get up early Saturday mornings and commune with nature and His heavenly Father. It was his time of devotion.

Well, this particular Saturday morning, he rose with the sun as he always did and went to the side of the cliff, looked out into the heavens, raised his hands, and worshipped. He closed his eyes and gave God the glory for all the beauty that He had created there. He stepped forward and began to sing his songs of praise when his foot slipped, and he fell off the mountain.

Well, as God would have it, there was a branch there, just beneath where he fell, and Deacon Jones was able to grab onto it. He held on as tight as he could and cried out to God for deliverance. "Help . . . help . . . help . . . "

The sound of his voice echoed through the mountainside. "Can anybody hear me . . . hear me . . . hear me . . . ?"

"Is anybody there . . . there . . . there . . . ?"

Hours passed, and Deacon Jones hung there crying and petitioning God. The sun rose to its highest peak, and he began to sweat. He prayed in earnest and bargained with God about all the things left for him to do and how he didn't want to die that way. The heat made his palms slippery, and he was worried about holding on much longer. Then suddenly the branch began to break. Deacon Jones felt his heart almost stop beating.

"Can anybody hear me . . . hear me . . . hear me?" he cried.

Then suddenly, a loud voice appeared to come from the heavens. It was deep and massive, and it shook the mountainside.

It said, "I hear you. If you hear my voice, let . . . go . . . of . . . the . . . limb."

The mountainside was silenced. Even the birds quieted down and waited. Finally, after a long pause, Deacon Jones responded. "Can anybody else hear me . . . hear me . . . hear me . . . ?"[1]

When I first heard that story (or joke), I laughed until my stomach ached. Then later I thought about the serious implications of what it actually meant. More often than not, that's exactly how we react to God's call for us to surrender. That's exactly how we respond to His outstretched hands when we are unsure. We want Him to help us and heal us, but we want Him to help and heal the way that fits our agenda.

We are tackling a lot these days. Stress, depression, and anxiety are destroying our faith in God and consequently our fellowship with Him. We have no idea of God's power and willingness to help us, if we would only surrender to Him. Surrender your pain. Surrender your addictions. Surrender your loss and desperation. Surrender your shattered hopes. Fully acknowledge the pain; experience and embrace the pain as it is right now, without pushing any part of it away or clinging to anything, and then release it to God.

> Fully acknowledge the pain; experience and embrace the pain as it is right now, without pushing any part of it away or clinging to anything, and then release it to God.

I'm not the brightest bulb in the chandelier. But I think, oftentimes, we delay healing in our lives when we depend on our limited understanding of our situations. We fuss about trying to lay down a plan of recovery or predict what would happen "if." We settle for mediocrity in our lives when we struggle through the hard times and find our own solutions.

Isaac Disraeli once said, "It is a wretched taste to be gratified with mediocrity when the excellent lies before us."

Everything outside of full surrender to God for our healing is mediocrity. Everything that involves wondering about what lies ahead in our journey is mediocrity. I invite you now to live in the present, where the excellent are before us. Our Father's loving hands, which provide healing, are the excellent. So close are they that peace is yours right now for the asking. So close are they that immediately, as Isaiah 30:15 says, "In quietness and confidence shall be your strength" (NKJV).

I have a friend named Nelson. Nelson has been redeemed from alcohol and drug addictions for more than two years. He attributes his new life to the healing powers of Jesus Christ. He's a carpenter by trade, and although he works with his hands, his mind moves more than a mile a minute.

I see him sometimes go so deep in thought that he barely knows that other people are in the room. He stands about five feet eleven inches tall with a worker's athletic build and has piercing hazel eyes that at times seem to be searching my soul for some great insight into life and the personality of God. More often than not, it's he who shares the wisdom. I have grown to love him dearly and look forward to our time together. Nelson owns and operates a home improvement and repair company, but it hasn't always been this way in his life.

He shared with me that he has been in and out of jail. He has had numerous traumas and failed relationships in his life, and he's been on a path of self-destruction. He told me that he had tried several times to "get his life together," but to no avail. It wasn't until he surrendered his pain and addictions to Jesus that things began to turn around for him. He said that the only way God was able to do anything in his life was when he was open and honest and surrendered.

His life has progressed beyond mediocrity. How many of us

can see things so clearly through the fog of our own desires and what we choose to believe?

Nelson told me the other day that, as he was working in someone's home, and after he'd finished the day's work, the homeowner offered him a cold beer. Nelson said he smiled and graciously refused. He explained to the homeowner that it wasn't his intent to be rude or anything; it's just that he couldn't have a beer because he's allergic. Every time he has a drink, he breaks out in handcuffs.

How many of us can be so vulnerable and so true to who we are without the shame, acknowledging our healing while allowing Christ to remove our guilt and the shame from our past pains and disappointments? I believe that Andy knows who he is and doesn't pretend to be anyone else. This man is living an authentic life of surrender to the Lord. He is giving away all of the good, the bad, and the real of his journey of healing.

Later in the day, we discussed recovery and God's role in it all. Nelson said that God has no role in recovery. *"God is healing."*

It took me a few days to process all that I heard from him, but I now understand how Nelson's experiences and mine merge. I understand how a survivor of a hurricane can relate to a drug addict who can relate to a victim of a terrorist attack who can relate to a rape victim who can relate to a mother who has lost her child to murder. As I've said before, the recovery journey belongs to us. But the healing, the completeness, the making whole is from God. Shalom.

And then we meet at the place of surrender.

Each of us, surrendering control of our lives, along with our urges and the reason for our urges, our fears and the reason for our fears, the understanding, or lack thereof, of the pain and trauma in our lives to God—that He might redeem us to Himself and heal. Each of us, being honest in our pain and telling God about it, even if that means shouting, is made whole.

He says, "Come to me, all you who are weary and burdened,

and I will give you rest. Take my yoke upon you and learn from me, for I am gentle and humble in heart, and you will find rest for your souls. For my yoke is easy and my burden is light" (Matthew 11:28-30). *For my yoke is easy . . . for my yoke is sooooooooooooo easy and my burden is light.*

Go to Him. Go to Daddy. Stand naked before the Lord, stripped of who you were. Take your troubles, take your concerns, take your loved ones, take your finances, take your pain and torment. Take the source of your fears and all that keeps you bound. Take it to Dad and find your rest. Only in His arms will you find comfort and strength enough to embrace your suffering and heal. Know that these are the times in our lives that deepen us. They teach us to pray. They make us wiser and gentler, full of hope and more like Him.

During my conversation with Nelson, I saw in his eyes a longing to know God and to be intimately more personal with Him. It inspired me. You see, Nelson was for me that day the personification of a surrendered life. His actions, more than his words, told a story of living the traumas and troubles, giving them to God and allowing something new to take place. Shalom.

Like Nelson, I could never have imagined the rich, rewarding life that I experience now without the Lord. Both of us have embarked on such a beautiful journey, an adventure of discovery; and a greater sense of freedom, authority, and energy now stirs within us.

I have learned from my new friend that perhaps God, after hearing all that we have to say to Him and years of our telling Him, sometimes quietly and other times in a loud voice, the demands of our lives and the deepest desires of our own hearts, making promises to Him that we seldom keep, uses our words of surrender to bring us closest to His heart.

I'm sure that the sweetest words to our heavenly Father are perhaps the simplest ones: "Yes, Lord."

Looking to Him makes life a lot more worth living through the storms, past the disappointments, and beyond the fears because we know we are headed straight into His arms.

So let me invite you now to stop and look around you without trying to fix anything. Simply notice what *is*, and realize that this is life, in all its chaos and its glory.

> Stop and look around you without trying to fix anything. Simply notice what *is*, and realize that this is life, in all its chaos and its glory.

And then surrender it. Be open.

At last, I propose to you that in matters of life and your relationship with Him, it is more about surrender than anything else and knowing that one day will find us in the presence of our almighty God and loving Father.

So as you rest tonight . . . when you close your eyes
Imagine that your Daddy is near.
Softly lay His pillow next to you and whisper to His ear,
"Sweet Father, thank you for the storms, for they bring me
  rainbows.
I honor you for the tears that wash despair.
Thank you for hope that brings healing
And the arms that show You care."

Will you pray with me?

Lord of peace,
    We say yes to all that You have planned for our lives, and
we receive with open arms.
    Amen.

Dance like nobody's watching; love
like you've never been hurt. Sing like
nobody's listening; live like it's heaven
on earth.

—MARK TWAIN

CHAPTER 17

LIVING FROM THE BEGINNING

Jerry was the kind of person that you just love to hate. He was always in a good mood and always had something positive to say. He sang in the mass choir at church on Sunday mornings and was, perhaps, loudest of all. When someone would ask him how he was doing, he would reply, "If I were any better, I would be twins!"

Jerry managed a small restaurant on the edge of town, which was always busy because people liked being called by their name. Jerry was a unique manager. Several waiters had followed him around from restaurant to restaurant because of his attitude.

He was a people person and a natural motivator. If an employee was having a bad day, Jerry was there telling the employee how to look on the positive side of the situation.

Seeing this style really made me curious. One day I went up to Jerry and asked him, "I don't get it! You can't be a positive person all of the time. How do you do it?"

Jerry replied, "Each morning I wake up and say to myself, I say, 'Jerry, you have two choices today. You can choose to be in a good mood, or you can choose to be in a bad mood.' I choose to be in a good mood. Each time something bad happens, I can choose to be a victim, or I can choose to learn from it. I choose to learn from it. Every time someone comes to me complaining, I can choose to accept their complaining, or I can point out the positive side of life. I choose the positive side of life."

"Yeah, right. It's not that easy," I protested.

"Yes, it is," Jerry said. "Life is all about choices. When you cut away all the junk, every situation is a choice. You choose how you react to situations. You choose how people will affect your mood. You choose to be in a good mood or a bad mood. You choose to be a good person or a stinker. The bottom line is it's your choice how you live life."

I reflected on what Jerry said.

Soon thereafter, I left the restaurant industry to start my own business. We lost touch, but I often thought about him when I made a choice about life instead of reacting to it.

Several years later, I heard that Jerry did something you are never supposed to do in a restaurant business: He left the back door open one morning while cleaning and was held up at gunpoint by three armed robbers.

While trying to open the safe, his hand, shaking from nervousness, slipped off the combination. The robbers panicked and shot him. Luckily, Jerry was found relatively soon after the shots were fired, and he was rushed to the local trauma center.

After eighteen hours of surgery and weeks of intensive care, Jerry was released from the hospital with fragments of the bullets still in his body.

I saw Jerry about six months after the accident. When I asked him how he was, he said, "If I were any better, I'd be twins. Want to see my scars?"

I declined to see his wounds, but I did ask him what had gone through his mind as the robbery took place. "The first thing that went through my mind was that I should have locked the back door," Jerry replied. "Then, as I lay on the floor, I remembered that I had two choices: I could choose to live, or I could choose to die. I chose to live."

"Weren't you scared? Did you lose consciousness?" I asked.

Jerry continued. "The paramedics were great. They kept telling me I was going to be fine. But when they wheeled me into the emergency room and I saw the expressions on the faces of the doctors and nurses, I got really scared. In their eyes I read, 'He's a dead man.' I knew I needed to take action."

"What did you do?" I asked.

"Well, there was a big, burly nurse shouting questions at me," said Jerry. "She asked if I was allergic to anything. 'Yes,' I replied. The doctors and nurses stopped working as they waited for my reply. The room was quiet except for the monitors. I took a deep breath and yelled, 'Bullets!' Over their laughter, I told them, 'I am choosing to live. Operate on me as if I am alive, not dead.'"

Jerry lived, thanks to the skill of his doctors, but also because of his amazing attitude. I learned from him that every day we have the choice to live fully . . . abundantly. Attitude, after all, is everything.[1]

Every day we have the choice to live fully . . . abundantly. This story speaks loud and clear to the fact that life is about living it to the fullest from your mind, body, and soul—at least from what I can see.

I believe that God calls us to live our lives as boldly as possible, with unrestricted access to joy. He tells us to live out loud, laugh out loud, and love out loud. Jesus said, "I am come that [you] might have life, and that [you] might have it more abundantly" (John 10:10, KJV). I want you to have the fullness of every breath that you breathe. You should love hard, until it hurts. You should live hard, until you can't deny life anymore.

Many of us experienced tragedy and got stuck there. We decided to live life more cautiously. We made some resolutions and some attempts to be more outgoing, but we never really got past the fear that if we live too boldly, we'll die with regrets.

I'm not sure about you, but at this point in my life, after having suffered the slings and arrows of outrageous fortune and having taken arms against the seas of troubles, the only way I'll regret anything at death is if I've never lived.

The only way I'll regret anything at death is if I've never lived.

I propose to you that God wants us to know that life is more than the breath we breathe. Life is a wholehearted and surrendered approach to embracing our experiences and participating in the movement of things around us. Living brings fulfillment and acceptance of the things that really matter. Boundaries disappear, our spirits open up to endless possibilities, and we enjoy abundant living. Gradually, the ability to trust steps in and the subtle art of loving without possessing becomes apparent. The art of caring without inhibitions is clear. The art of commitment without condition is luminous, and we are alive!

We stop holding on to so much, and we make fewer demands on breathing and more on life. We begin to relax and ease more into the flow of things. We delight in the good things of life when they are present and accept change without protest when they end. The heart opens wider as it learns there is nothing to lose.

We are only here for a short time, my friend. But even as this life is not the promise or the one to covet, our time here should be exciting, not inhibiting. We should not make time for playing mental and emotional games with those we love. We should not beat around the bush with those that we want to love. We should not stay shackled to our burdens.

Be allergic to that way of thinking, as Jerry was to those bullets. Move beyond what has been the norm, and decide to do more than just exist. There is a beautiful world out there filled with power for living. God wants us to grab hold of it and go for it! He wants us to live beyond what we see.

The abundant life is within our reach if only we will drink deeply of living water, fill our hearts with love, and create of our lives a masterpiece.

Instead of clinging to the way things used to be, or how we want them to be, I invite you to live in the present. Accept all the dissatisfactions and sorrows of the human heart as merely one aspect of a comprehensive work of art.

Rain down on us, Father, that Your healing waters would wash over the shore, cover our journey, and flood our lives with the peace of God.

In my travels, I have heard it said that the only happy people are dead people. But I disagree.

There are people, like Jerry, who walk in joy and radiate happiness. They live lives of abundance, and they live.

Even I now walk outside a lot more and play in the sunshine. I spend more time now in the park and on singles weekends and a lot less time dusting. (My friend Andy noted that for me, just the other day.) I'm sitting on the back deck and admiring the view without fussing about the weeds in the garden or the neighbor's barking dog or even the fact that the house needs painting. I'm spending more time with my family and friends and less time in the office, at church group meetings, or on the phone.

I believe that whenever and wherever possible, life should be surrendered and lived and delighted in, not endured or struggled through. I'm asking God to give me wisdom in the little things like finding a moment in a song and letting it be mine and letting go. I'm not "saving" anything; I'm baking cakes and using the good dishes for every special event, like losing a pound, bathing the dog, and remembering to pick up toilet paper before a big storm. *I wish, maybe, someday,* and *one of these days* have lost their grip on my vocabulary.

> I believe that whenever and wherever possible, life should be surrendered and lived and delighted in, not endured or struggled through.

I understand now, as my mother did, to live unashamed before the Lord because life ends as quickly as it begins.

The message here is another effortless one. We cannot afford to allow the traumas and tragedies of life to limit our lives. As long as we're breathing, we've been given the go-ahead by God Himself to live.

This really is a good life. In this life, we get to have kindergarten parties and receive Valentine's Day cards from our friends. We get to feel the butterflies in our stomach when we fall in love for the first time and run to the phone to hear a familiar voice on the other end. In this life, we get to experience the headaches from too much chocolate, the annoyances from publicly used cell phones, the nightmares from scary old movies, and more importantly, we get to live this wild and crazy ride that ends just as suddenly as it begins.

In this life, we get to dance. . . .

Daddy,
My prayer tonight is for my sisters and brothers who yet weep.
It is for those who are operating in life as if they are dead. I
pray that, as they begin to process all that they have exposed
here in these pages, You would give them the faith to trust You
in the face of all mysteries, the love and power to glorify Your
name, wisdom to call upon You, and courage to live life . . .
abundantly.

Let it be so.
Amen.

Be faithful until death, and I will give you
the crown of life.

—Revelation 2:10, nkjv

CHAPTER 18

IT'S GONNA BE WORTH IT

I am persuaded that my mission in life is to fight for souls for the
Kingdom. It's rewarding to see lives changed and hope renewed. In
fact, the best part of my day is when I meet a reader who shares a
story of restored great expectations from something that I've said.
Not much is better than that.

I enjoy hearing of their great escapes and tales of survival.
I appreciate the honesty from them and the trust that they place
in me by opening their hearts and revealing their deepest pains,
fears—and yes—even desires.

Each of us has at least one story about our life's moment. If we have experienced any painful event at all, we can tell you when and where it was that our particular universe collapsed around us and when it was that we made the decision to live again. We have our coming-of-age stories, our greatest-lessons stories, and our best-times-of-our-lives stories. I think for the most part we even fashion our lives around those tales, and they become the sum of who we are.

We have watched, listened, laughed; undoubtedly, we have shed a few tears at what has been. We have looked back and remembered the good, the bad, and all those who have gone before us, leaving their mark on our hearts, inspiring us with new dreams and motivating us to a deeper faith in God. Our life's sufferings have been so rich and intense, so steeped in God's grace, that we tend to like trading them. They inevitably lead to endless discussions that steer us toward the appreciation of life being worth it all . . . and it is, really. For with the fullness of time, we receive the fullness of grace and truth. Is there a greater reward?

In the meantime, I believe that this life is one long experience of living and learning . . . one thing after another. We live a little, we learn a lot. We live a lot, and we learn that much more. And the lessons we learn through enduring our journeys—or stories, if you will—become gifts that we present to the Lord in the everlasting.

The Bible describes these gifts as crowns: the crown of life, which rewards faithfulness and perseverance during trials (James 1:12; Revelation 2:10); the crown of glory, which rewards those who shepherd God's people from a pure heart (1 Peter 5:1-4); the crown of righteousness, which rewards those who love and long for the Lord's appearing (2 Timothy 4:8); and the crown of rejoicing, the soul winner's crown (1 Thessalonians 2:19).

I decided a few years ago that I would wear the crown of rejoicing for my Father's good pleasure. And so my life, my stories, and my living now are about giving . . . all of me. You see, I've lived and survived a lot during my life journey thus far, and thankfully,

I've learned a thing or two as well. Each experience has birthed in me a greater light of love for my Father and a deeper burden for the souls of His people.

It's amazing how wide open my heart has become to desiring to be "invisible" in order that He can be seen.

And so I write, in hopes that I might encourage you through living this particular story or pain in your life and encourage you upward toward the everlasting. That's the only thing that makes it all worth it, the "race toward a rendezvous with God."

> Brothers, I do not consider myself yet to have taken hold of it. But one thing I do: Forgetting what is behind and straining toward what is ahead, I press on toward the goal to win the prize for which God has called me heavenward in Christ Jesus. (Philippians 3:13-14)

Again, I pray that the books I write contain one word, one sound, or one picture that will point you in the direction of hopefulness and the realization that your living is not in vain. Your tears are not unseen, and your sufferings are not for naught. Your story will one day take you to the place where you can finally claim your own crown.

Finding that strong sense of purpose in life, though neither easy nor automatic, is what God wants for us. We then love harder, live better, and have better relationships. Our priorities shift, and we appreciate time spent, time lost, and the creation of the best stories of our lives.

Martin Luther said that man should suffer his crosses in life patiently and "know that it is good and profitable for him."

My son, Eliot, and I recently spoke about these very things. We relived a few of my glamour moments and discussed some of his life experiences. We talked about how I've raised him and how God raises His children. Eliot made several good points, but his most profound was about finishing strong in life and about the sum of all life's sufferings—or "spankings"—being the map to a waiting treasure. He wrote a story for me. In it, he shared his insight about suffering, which, with his permission, I'm sharing with you.

THE BEST SPANKINGS OF MY LIFE

> *It has been said that at least three times in a person's life, they are faced with life-changing decisions, or an epiphany. I am living proof that this is 100 percent accurate. After thirteen years of uninterrupted spankings, I have concluded that my mother is a superhero. She has supernatural abilities such as rubber arms, deadly aim, the sixth sense, and rock slippers. My mom could give a spanking from three blocks away and around the corner.*
>
> *Before I go any further, let me take you to back in the day when I started really getting into trouble.*
>
> *I remember as if it were yesterday. I was five or six years old. Mom had just picked me up from school, and we were on our way home. We took the bus that day. You see, my mom worked nonstop, so when she finally had a break, she stayed home until it was time to pick me up. She would get me, we would go out to eat, come home, do my homework, and then watch TV together. This woman was my mom, but she had a replacement that I came to know as Leslie, or the makeup lady.*
>
> *Now, any other day, the school bus would drop me off at my babysitter's house or at my grandmother's. Mom would always call from work around the time she knew I should have been where I was supposed to be. She wanted to make sure that everything was perfect; anything less was unacceptable. Mom was great. She was loving and forgiving.*
>
> *Leslie was the makeup lady. And it always seemed that this*

woman would give me most of my spankings. That's why this occurrence came as such a surprise for me. Back to the story.

Mom and I were on our way home. We were laughing and talking together, and she kept giving me the "loving mommy" look. The school day had been relatively short, all the kids finished early, and the teacher gave us each candy.

Did I mention that I have a fast metabolism?

We were on a bus with some nuns, and I had gotten so hyperactive that I couldn't control myself. I was screaming, yelling, and being rude to my mom. She kept telling me to quiet down, but I didn't. It seemed that the more I did it, the more I enjoyed it.

Mom got quiet. The nuns and all the other people on the bus stared with obvious disapproval. Mom didn't say a word.

Soon we got off the bus, and I felt a strong tug at my pants, immediately followed by a sting to my bum like no other. I screamed but couldn't seem to get away from the pain. Mom gave me a spanking right there in front of all of those people. I heard the nuns screaming, "That's right, ma'am, discipline him in the way of the Lord!" At that moment, I knew that my first epiphany had come. The way of the Lord really does hurt.

When I got older, I remember laughing with my cousins about life and the spankings that we endured. We shared stories that were unbelievable, mostly because they weren't true. They ranged from shoe whippings to long stares, then to long-armed whippings, to my story about the bus. I have others, many others. But there was for me, central to each of my stories, a mysterious makeup lady and the way of the Lord.

Another time I was staying with my grandma while Mom worked. Grandma had been watching television all day, it was hot outside, and her family room was a mess. I'd tried to get her to fix me something good to eat all day. All I had had was Pop-Tarts and cereal. Mom always made hot food. I wanted hot food.

Finally, I'd had enough. I walked boldly into the room where Grandma was, walked up to the television, turned it off, and demanded she fix me something hot to eat. I told her, "Fix it, or I'm calling Mom." (Did I mention that I was only about nine years old?)

Grandma thought it was cute, so she never told Mom. Somehow, a few years later, makeup lady found out, and it wasn't pleasant. Did you know that there is no statute of limitations on spankings? Mom told me then that she had to "train me up." Her training me up seemed a lot worse than boot camp. She said that wherever I messed up was where she was coming with correction. She never lied.

My final story is the most recent of the many, many spankings I endured in my life. It was six years ago. I was just beginning to get more popular at my junior high school. That's right. I was a teenager. I was picking my own clothes and making my own fashion decisions. "Hello hip-hop fashions, and good-bye Tommy Hilfiger."

This particular day, I wore a blue shirt, blue jeans, and a hat tilted to the left and slanting downward. I ate my breakfast like any other day and was about to go outside to catch my bus. I said good-bye to my mom and tried to escape the house.

"Eliot! Take that hat off of your head like that. It looks too thuggish." As I passed her bedroom, I made a motion as if I was removing the hat. I was going to give her the satisfaction of feeling right about something and then I'd leave. "Okay, Mom," I said as I began to leave.

"Eliot!"

What now? I thought. "Yes, Mom?"

"Didn't I tell you to take that off your head?"

"I did," I said. I was annoyed, and I made an "I'm so annoyed at you, woman" face where she couldn't see me.

"Eliot, get over here," she yelled. I went into her room, and

the door shut the exact same moment that my heart stopped. The rest of the beating was a blur.

For the rest of the day, I kept wondering how she knew that I lied and that I didn't remove the hat. I couldn't concentrate all day. The spanking that started my day kept coming back to my mind. Finally, I just accepted the fact that she knew me so well that she had gained the sixth sense. Besides, it really didn't matter how she knew. I had that one coming.

When I got home, I apologized for lying and for being disrespectful. I gave Mom a hug, and we watched TV together for the rest of the evening.

It was brought to my attention while writing this for her that in our old house, where that spanking took place, there was a small mirror behind me in Mom's room, strategically placed so that she could watch the front door from her bed.

Mom is Mom today, and makeup lady is no more. However, I still laugh when I think about it, because Mom has no clue that I know she is a superhero. She still grabs hot plates with the greatest of ease, she senses yard sales from miles away, she knows everything about girls and a good amount of information about me, and most of what she says these days makes perfect sense.

Mom's a superhero, not like Santa, who is around only in the good times, or the tooth fairy, who is there only in the night; not like the Easter bunny, who is only there when it's nice weather. Mothers are always there . . . in the way of the Lord. And the way of the Lord includes spankings when there is an immediate need and a need for periods of hard learning, both of which are followed by a wonderful gift of time and grace. For me, it was long afternoons spent watching television with my mom.

Years ago, Mom told me that she would never let anyone hurt me, not even me. She kept her word. I am almost nineteen years old now. I'm in college, doing well, and the way of the Lord has kept me from ever being in serious trouble or being arrested. I have never used drugs, I have never hit a girl, I have never spit on a baby or killed anyone. I have never disrespected a person in authority or been rude to an elderly person. I open doors for young ladies and carry Mom's grocery bags. I control myself, and "self" does not rule over me.

I remember recently thinking to myself, All those spankings that I endured over the years and over the littlest things, for what? I have begun to realize, in life, God doesn't do things or allow our sufferings for His pleasure, or for our comfort, but rather because they are necessary. I have never run a race in which I could immediately see the finish line, but when my endurance is fading and my hope begins to shake in my stomach, I persevere because I know that line is there, and I am determined to cross it. It is the encouragement of finishing the race.[1]

At first glance, this "lessons learned" story from a growing boy pales in the light of what we learn from surviving hurricanes, tornadoes, cancer, and the like. But as we delve deeper, we understand that pain is pain no matter the extent of suffering, and therefore our focus should not be on the varying degrees of our circumstance. It should be on what is birthed through that specific ordeal. That's where God's investment is.

Eliot makes a valid point when he says that "God doesn't do things or allow our sufferings for His pleasure, or for our comfort, but rather because they are necessary." Necessary to humble us and bring us closer to Him—necessary to build our character and make us more like Him—necessary to change our perspective from the natural to the supernatural where our battles are fought and won—necessary to increase the worth of our treasures and the jewels in our crowns.

The Bible says, "Consider it pure joy, my brothers, whenever you face trials of many kinds, because you know that the testing of your faith develops perseverance. . . . Blessed is the man who perseveres under trial, because when he has stood the test, he will receive the crown of life that God has promised to those who love him" (James 1:2-3, 12).

"When he has stood the test, he will receive the crown of life." God so much wants us to be faithful, to stand and endure through our sufferings, that He offers a tremendous reward! He wants to place crowns upon our heads in celebration of overcoming. He wants us to be pleased in our journeys and press on through struggles. With our eyes lifted up and focused on Him, He wants us to stand.

No amount of despair in our lives can alter the reality of things, or stain the joy of the promises of God, which are always there for us. The fact is that God has invited us to forget ourselves on purpose and push past the "commas" we place in the middle of our stories so that we can face life by looking past it and seeing the everlasting, where great promise awaits.

> No amount of despair in our lives can alter the reality of things, or stain the joy of the promises of God, which are always there for us.

Eliot's story picks up that point very well. He makes it crystal clear that whether pain comes by our hands or the hands of another or a natural occurrence, we will have our lot of suffering in this life. There is no escaping that. But if we receive our trials and do not fight against them, as Christ has instructed us, they give us the characteristics necessary to fight the good fight against sin. They build our endurance so that we have what it takes to run a good race and receive our perfect gift of life. The question is how to benefit individually unto our everlasting glory and happiness in heaven.

Paul wrote along similar lines . . .

> I have fought a good fight, I have finished my course, I have kept the faith: Henceforth there is laid up for me a crown

of righteousness, which the Lord, the righteous judge, shall give me at that day: and not to me only, but unto all them also that love his appearing. (2 Timothy 4:7, KJV)

How sweet is that reward? How much easier would our struggles be if we could focus on that prize rather than the thing that brings the pain?

God offers us the most precious treasure and the most wonderful gift of all. He gives us the fullness of life here and the promise of eternal life after death.

(How great is Thy presence, O God, that I yearn to be with You always!)

For now, here we dwell—not one of us is exempt from the gift. Therefore none of us is exempt from the suffering. Our common state remains living the stories we tell about ourselves and others, and the meaning of all that life is.

And God, having caused the whole universe to be alive with His life, consistently reaches out to get our attention and to reveal Himself to us, to communicate with us, to allow in our lives the enormity of some circumstances, in order to stir an awakening within us and the desire to know Him more. But we must, as Eliot says, "finish the race." Finish strong.

For those who do, God's rewards are more wonderful than any human mind has ever been able to imagine. His promise is that "No eye has seen, no ear has heard, no mind has conceived what God has prepared for those who love him" (1 Corinthians 2:9).

So endure, my friends! Be strong and courageous. Hold fast to the experiences and create the stories. Know with the knowing that expands beyond any known boundary that one day it's going to be worth it to walk the streets of gold and plant gardens outside the mansions that wait. It's gonna be worth it to sit and chat with those of old and sing songs with the angels' chorus. It's gonna be worth it to see His beautiful face and finally sup with Him.

So as for me and my house, *we will serve the Lord.* And no amount of tragedy will keep us from that. For how long is a lifetime on earth, and what does it compare with life over the veil, or an eternity of endless delight? In the grand scheme of things, how long can sorrow actually last, and what does it profit us to suffer to no good end?

Even if we get to heaven all beaten and battered from life, what a day of celebration it will be when we get there! Alas, my friends, this life, packed with all things that make it exciting and wonderful—chocolate and puppies and death and struggles and good movies and bad hair days and terror and AIDS and cancer and crooked hats and spankings and hundred-year-old grandmas and so much more—is the road that takes us there. The happy times that we experience now are as significant to our journeys as the suffering. They are our stories, and they inspire us.

So hold on a bit longer. Live bravely and with great anticipation. Press on with a determined heart and more than a little courage each time to wrench yourself loose from the clutches of your sufferings. Hold fast to hope of the everlasting with a purposeful grip, and imagine finishing strong—actually living forever in the presence of the Almighty God.

> Hold fast to hope of the everlasting with a purposeful grip, and imagine finishing strong—actually living forever in the presence of the Almighty God.

Finally, about life . . . Eliot decided that his spankings kept him from the streets and that they made him a better young man. As his journey deepens, he remains steadfast in his commitment to being that better godly man. My son's hopes are for the crown of life.

Me? I am persuaded that my mission in life is to fight for souls for the Kingdom. I decided a few years ago that I would wear the crown of rejoicing for my Father's good pleasure. And so my life, my stories, and my living now are about giving . . . all of me.

So . . . you? What have you decided?

Heavenly Father,

I thank You for allowing pain to enter our lives that we might know that You have grace enough to comfort us. Let our sufferings be understood as necessary roughness, building endurance for this journey. Help us, Lord, to keep moving through life and to keep standing when the winds blow. Fix our focus upward on the treasure that awaits us, so that we are motivated to keep fighting against doubt and sin. I bow to You, dear Lord, and I thank You with my sincerest heart, for the perfect treasure of real life that begins with You when life here ends. I ask now for Your glory and for the sake of building the Kingdom that You would strengthen my brothers and sisters and those who are weak. Send Your angels to fight in their stead and strengthen them for the battle.

We thank You for Your hearing ears and for Your responsive heart.

Even so, come, Lord Jesus.
Amen.

CHAPTER 19

FINALLY

The Everlasting

You have arrived at this place, at this moment in time, and you are still wondering and still searching. Your heart, where you live, has been broken, and you have no idea how to pick up the pieces. Somewhere in the course of your living, your life was interrupted by something that never was supposed to happen. You have lived something so painful that it has brought you to this book and questions about God and how to heal.

I feel for you. I once lived there too.

I suppose that, in the light of who you are, there can be

seen some hint of a small bit of shame and uncertainty about the whys and the final leg of your life's journey. I imagine that you still remember it like it was yesterday. You probably still smell whatever it was that lingered in the air, and on some level, hope is fading.

I believe that this book in your hands right now is no coincidence. I believe that this book in your hands right now is providence. I pray for the eyes of your understanding that you might find clarity through these final pages or soon after.

> *Master,*
> *Once again, I approach Your throne with great admiration and expectation. I recognize and acknowledge the fact that You are the holy One, sovereign Lord, the great I AM, and Creator of all. I worship Your name and bow to Your authority, asking that, if it is Your will to do so, You would form these words into darts that pierce our hearts with truth and an awakening to You and to the reality and promise of the everlasting.*
> *I pray that this is Your will.*
> *Let it be so and let it be done, according to Your power.*
> *Amen.*

I don't know exactly what life is or how to explain those elements that I do know; however, I'm sure that immediately after death it will be crystal clear to all of us.

Recently there has been an explosion of interest in the things of God, namely, heaven. ABC News and other stations have aired programs on how to get there and who goes. News magazines have interviewed religious leaders, and each of them has pointed at a Bible verse or two and fumbled about trying to make it clear to nonbelievers. I guess, for me, the biggest disturbance about both programs was that nobody addressed the real question: Is there really life after death?

Now, before I jump off this limb, I'd like to go on the record with this disclaimer: I believe that life does not begin until death.

A few years ago, I read somewhere that several atheists had posed a scenario to a few believers about heaven and God. The theory was that life is like a roller-coaster ride. They suggested that at the end of life, you find yourself in a roller-coaster car, passing through a long and dark tunnel. I suppose for the sake of making it interesting they said that the tracks take you up and down a few modest bumps, splashing through water, then your car is brought to a halt. You then are caused to remember your life. You remember the time before you were born when you first began your ride, you remember some of the major decisions in your life, during your ride, and unless you had a remarkable life, in an instant you see how silly you were in life, misjudging what was important and what was unimportant. That is called the "Revelation."

Finally, you get off the ride at the same place where you got on, and it starts again. Now, if that is true, life has no purpose and it lets us all off the hook.

But what if they're wrong?

Just suppose for a moment that all the good things you've ever heard about Jesus were not true. Can you imagine what life would be like with no chance or hope of anything beyond now? What if we simply close our eyes and all that exists for us ceases to exist for us? What would be the reason for living, if everything ended the moment we die?

Now suppose again that every good deed goes unnoticed and every bad one goes unpunished. Why search for truth and reality if the Word of God is a lie? What if we simply suffer to no avail—when it's over, it simply ends? Why be good if there is no eventual reward? At the first level of understanding, it is because you can only really be good if there is no reward. At the second

level of understanding—which trumps the first, obliterating it—
we should be good for its own sake: good for goodness' sake. If
that's all, then there is nothing else.

What, then, would be the reason for praying for the best, if
life is a game of chance?

I propose to you that life is neither cosmic nor theory. It is
hope. God is neither science nor conjecture. God is faith.

I'm sure you've heard these positions before and have by now
certainly formed your own argument to defend the faith. Relax.
Nobody can either prove or disprove heaven. And I won't attempt
to, either. The choice to believe or not to believe is each individual's
decision.

What I seek to do here is simply ask that you open your mind
to the possibility that all of the sufferings that you experience in
life, all of the pain and misunderstanding amounts to a great release
one day in the everlasting. One day, it's going to be worth it! In
Romans 8:18, Paul states his attitude toward life: "I consider that
the sufferings of this present time are not worthy to be compared
with the glory which shall be revealed in us" (NKJV).

No one can be convinced about the everlasting or talked into
faith in God. We love by invitation, and we believe by faith. Our
lives—inclusive of the ups and the downs and the pitfalls—will lead us, individually, to that juncture where we choose. For some, heartbreak and pain will be the road where He is found. For others, it will be a quiet song. And then, finally, there will always be those of us who require tragedy and a dark night of the soul to bring us to His feet.

> There will always be those of us who require tragedy and a dark night of the soul to bring us to His feet.

Nevertheless, I believe that for each of us, heaven is the
place where we'll meet Him face-to-face—and He will reveal His
glory—face to face—and we will be like Him—face to face—and

the purpose of this ride, this journey, complete with its pain and joy, will be revealed to us: His purpose for our lives has always been life . . . the everlasting.

Now, suppose if you will, that all the good things you've heard about Jesus are gospel. Can you imagine what life should be like full of His promises of hope of resurrection? What if we close our eyes and open them once more in a place of beauty and rest? What would be the reason for living hopeless, if life began the moment we die?

Now just suppose for a moment a place of perfect beauty and peace. Where there is love, ethnic diversity, cultural awareness, food for thought, and acceptance. Imagine songs of joy and hope and a great celebration of overcoming . . . a party.

John describes an entire city of transparent gold. He tells us that the walls of the new city are precious jewels. The gates are twelve single pearls. The city itself and its streets are pure gold, yet like transparent glass (see Revelation 21:18, 19, 21, paraphrased). And the whole city is lighted by the glory of God.

My vision

There is an open sky, and people are laughing and talking together all day. Our actions and the things we speak of bring honor to God. He is pleased by our lifestyles, and He dines with us. We sit at times in the garden of original intent and commune with our brothers and sisters of old. There is even more laughing and comparisons of our personal journeys. I show my battle scars and John the Baptist shows his. I speak of my long exodus from Tower One, and Moses shares his own tale of escape. I talk briefly of being homeless, and Jonah quickly smiles my way. I pull out my books and boast of lyrical writings, and Paul laughs.

Finally, we share a tall, cold glass of lemonade beneath a blossoming fig tree, and all is well.

Will you come?

Heavenly Father,
Lord, bring them in. For all these and for all of our world,
I pray for the fire and the dance, the peace and the laughter,
the passion and the joy of having not only drawn near to Your
Kingdom, but of having entered it. For not only having tasted
Your goodness, but having been filled.

Bring them in, Father, those who seek and desire to give
their lives to You. My prayer is that souls are saved and sin
is abandoned that we might together share in the joys of the
everlasting.

Be found, my Father, by all who seek You now. I ask it
in Jesus' name and according to His will.

Amen.

MY FINAL WORDS OF ENCOURAGEMENT

Closure . . . ain't it great?

Finally, you've arrived. You've cried. You've asked why. You've spent some time alone with our Father, you've tried some journaling exercises, and you've surrendered—now what?

Now is the time to choose whether you live in glorious hope or futile hopelessness. It is your decision whether to struggle through this season of pain or lie peacefully in His arms, being held.

You came here looking for closure, for something that was bigger than anything else in your life. You came in response to an attraction to some wordless possibility or in hopes of finding refreshing, healing waters to soothe the memory of your dark night of the soul, birth in you a life change, and give you great expectations for your healing.

I pray that instead you've received, and now will begin to notice, the tiny miracles that effect spiritual growth in you.

I pray for your journey.

Heavenly and dearest Father,

I have ended this book here, but Your love goes beyond what I have written. For many, this is the point in the journey where recovery ends and healing begins. Thank You. Thank You because You are our Father and You care. I ask now, of a caring Father, that You would give Your children the assurance that You are mightier than the sword of sufferings and that nothing has power but You, unless they make it so. We need You in our dark hours. We need You in the light of salvation. Come, Lord Jesus, and make us whole. Restore each of us to the place of Your original intent . . . peaceful in a garden, fellowshipping with You, and being held.

Thank You, Father, for hearing us this day. We receive now our transformations as we move forward slowly and expectantly, anticipating great things from the people we will meet in the mirror each new day.

Thank You, Father, that You have already answered before we opened our mouths to speak. Hear now the individual prayers from the hearts of Your children, even when there are no words. Listen, O Lord, to the hearts.

Grant us now strength for the journey to endure even unto the end, where we will gather together with You and the saints in a beautiful day of celebration . . . even unto the everlasting. Keep our hope in You.

"Now to Him who is able to keep you from stumbling, and to present you faultless before the presence of His glory with exceeding joy, to God our Savior, who alone is wise, be glory and majesty, dominion and power, both now and forever. Amen" (Jude 1:24-25, NKJV).

Go in peace. *Shalom.*

AN AFTERTHOUGHT

Second to Paul, A. W. Tozer provides some of my favorite reading material. I found this a few years ago in an old document library, and it has been a light for me ever since. I'd like to be wise enough one day to write as these men did. On second thought, I'd like to be wise enough one day to discuss their writings with them.

In the meantime, be encouraged.

"FIVE VOWS FOR SPIRITUAL POWER" BY A. W. TOZER

Some people object to taking vows, but in the Bible you will find many great men of God directed by covenants, promises, vows and pledges. The psalmist was not averse to the taking of vows:

"Thy vows are upon me, O God," he said. "I will render my praises unto thee" (Psalm 56:12).

My counsel in this matter is that if you are really concerned about spiritual improvement—the gaining of new power, new life, new joy and new personal revival within your heart—you will do well to make certain vows and proceed to keep them. If you should fail, go down in humility and repent and start over. But always keep these vows before you. They will help harmonize your heart with the vast powers that flow out and down from the throne where Christ sits at the right hand of God.

A carnal man refuses the discipline of such commitments. He says, "I want to be free. I don't want to lay any vows upon myself; I don't believe in it. It is legalism." Well, let me paint a picture of two men.

One of them will not take vows. He will not accept any responsibility. He wants to be free. And he is free, in a measure— just as a tramp is free. The tramp is free to sit on a park bench by day, sleep on a newspaper by night, get chased out of town on Thursday morning, and find his way up a set of creaky stairs in some flophouse on Thursday night. Such a man is free, but he is also useless. He clutters up the world whose air he breathes.

Let's look at another man—maybe a president or prime minister or any great man who carries upon himself the weight of government. Such men are not free. But in the sacrifice of their freedom they step up in power. If they insist upon being free, they can be free, just like the tramp. But they choose rather to be bound.

There are many religious tramps in the world who will not be bound by anything. They have turned the grace of God into personal license. But the great souls are ones who have gone reverently to God with the understanding that in their flesh dwells no good thing. And they know that without God's enablement any vows taken would be broken before sundown. Nevertheless, believing in God, reverently they took certain sacred vows. This is the way to spiritual power.

Now there are five vows I have in mind that we do well to make and keep. The first is: Deal thoroughly with sin. Sin has been driven underground these days and has come up with a new name and face. You may be subjected to this phenomenon in the schools. Sin is called by various fancy names—anything but what it really is. For example, men don't get under conviction any more; they get a guilt complex. Instead of confessing their guilt to God and getting rid of it, they lie down on a couch and try to tell a man who ought to know better all about themselves. It comes out after a while that they were deeply disappointed when they were two years old or some such thing. That's supposed to make them better.

The whole thing is ridiculous, because sin is still the ancient enemy of the soul. It has never changed. We've got to deal firmly with sin in our lives. Let's remember that. "The kingdom of God is not meat and drink," said Paul, "but righteousness, and peace, and joy in the Holy Ghost" (Romans 14:17). Righteousness lies at the door of the kingdom of God. "The soul that sinneth, it shall die" (Ezekiel 18:4, 20).

This is not to preach sinless perfection. This is to say that every known sin is to be named, identified and repudiated, and that we must trust God for deliverance from it, so that there is no more sin anywhere in our lives. It is absolutely necessary that we deal thus, because God is a holy God and sin is on the throne of the world.

So don't call your sins by some other name. If you're jealous, call it jealousy. If you tend to pity yourself and feel that you are not appreciated, but are like a flower born to blush unseen and waste your sweetness on the desert air, call it what it is—self-pity.

There is resentfulness. If you're resentful, admit it. I have met people who live in a state of sputtering indignation most of the time. I know of a preacher who acts like a hen thrown out of the nest. He keeps running in all directions clucking and complaining—somebody is always doing him wrong. Well, if you have got that spirit, you must deal with it now. You must get that out of you. The blood of Jesus Christ cleanses from all sin. Instead of covering it up and trying to find a Greek marginal rendering somewhere to hide it under, call it by the right name, and get rid of it by the grace of God.

And then there is your temper. Don't call it indignation. Don't try to christen it by some other name. Call it what it is. Because if you have a bad temper you will either get rid of it or it will get rid of much of your spirituality and most of your joy.

So let's deal with sin thoroughly. Let's be perfectly candid. God loves candid people.

Now the second vow is: Never own anything. I do not mean by this that you cannot have things. I mean that you ought to get delivered from this sense of possessing them. This sense of possessing is what hinders us. All babies are born with their fists clenched, and it seems to me it means: "This is mine!" One of the first things is "mine" in an angry voice. That sense of "This is mine" is a very injurious thing to the spirit. If you can get rid of it so that you have no feeling of possessing anything, there will come a great sense of freedom and liberty into your life.

Now don't think that you must sell all that you have and give it to charity. No, God will let you have your car and your business, your practice and your position, whatever it may be, provided you understand that it is not yours at all, but His, and all you are doing is just working for Him. You can be restful about it then, because we never need to worry about losing anything that belongs to someone else. If it is yours, you're always looking in your hand to see if it's still there. If it's God's you no longer need to worry about it.

Let me point out some things you'll have to turn over to God. Property is one thing. Some of the dear Lord's children are being held back because there's a ball and chain on their legs. If it's a man, it's his big car and fine home. If it's a woman it's her china and her Louis XIV furniture and all the rest. Take that vase for instance. There it stands, and if anybody knocked it off and broke it the poor owner would probably lose five years from her life!

The third vow is this: Never defend yourself. We're all born with a desire to defend ourselves. And if you insist upon defending yourself, God will let you do it. But if you turn the defense of yourself over to God He will defend you. He told Moses once, in Exodus 23:22: "I will be an enemy unto thine enemies and an adversary to thine adversaries."

A long time ago, the Lord and I went through the 23rd chapter of Exodus together and He gave it to me. For thirty years now, it has been a source of untold blessing to my life. I don't have to fight. The Lord does the fighting for me. And He'll do the same for you. He will be an enemy to your enemy and an adversary to your adversary, and you'll never need to defend yourself.

What do we defend? Well, we defend our service, and particularly we defend our reputation. Your reputation is what people think you are, and if a story gets out about you the big temptation is to try to run it down. But you know, running down the source of a story is a hopeless task. Absolutely hopeless! It's like trying to find the bird after you've found the feather on your lawn. You can't do it. But if you'll turn yourself wholly over to the Lord He will defend you completely and see to it that no one will harm you. "No weapon that is formed against thee shall prosper," he says, and "every tongue that shall rise against thee in judgment thou shalt condemn" (Isaiah 54:17).

Henry Suso was a great Christian of other days. Once he was seeking what some Christians have told me they are seeking—to know God better. Let's put it like this: you are seek-ing to have a religious awakening within your spirit that will thrust you farther out into the deep things of God. Well, as Henry Suso was seeking God, people started telling evil stories about the man, and it grieved him so that he wept bitter tears and had great sorrow of heart.

Then one day he looked out the window and saw a dog playing on the lawn. The dog had a mat, and kept picking the mat up, tossing it over his shoulder, running and getting it, tossing it some more, picking it up and tossing it again. God said to Henry Suso, "That mat is your reputation, and I am letting the dogs of sin tear your reputation to shreds and toss it all over the lawn for your own good. One of these days things will change."

And things did change. It was not very long before people who were tearing his reputation were confounded, and Suso rose into a place that made him a power in his day and a great bless-ing still to those who sing his hymns and read his works.

Next vow: Never pass anything on about anybody else that will hurt him. "Love covers a multitude of sins" (1 Peter 4:8). The talebearer has no place in God's favor. If you know some-thing that would hinder or hurt the reputation of one of God's children, bury it forever. Find a little garden out back—a little spot somewhere—and when somebody comes around with an evil story, take it out and bury it, and say, "Here lies in peace the story about my brother." God will take care of it. "With what judgment ye judge, ye shall be judged" (Matthew 7:2).

If you want God to be good to you, you are going to have to be good to His children. You say, "That's not grace." Well, grace gets you into the kingdom of God. That is unmerited favor. But after you are seated at the Father's table He expects to teach you table manners. And He won't let you eat unless you obey the etiquette of the table. And what is that? The etiquette of the table is that you don't tell stories about the brother who is sitting at the table with you—no matter what his denomination, or nationality or background.

Our next vow is: Never accept any glory. God is jealous of His glory and He will not give His glory to another. He will not even share His glory with another. It is quite natural, I should say, for people to hope that maybe their Christian service will give them a chance to display their talents. True, they want to serve the Lord. But they also want other people to know they are serving the Lord. They want to have a reputation among the saints. That is very dangerous ground—seeking a reputation among the saints. It's bad enough to seek a reputation in the world, but it's worse to seek a reputation among the people of God. Our Lord gave up His reputation, and so must we.

Meister Eckhart once preached a sermon on Christ cleansing the temple. He said, "Now there was nothing wrong with those men selling and buying there. There was nothing wrong with exchanging money there; it had to be. The sin lay in their doing it for profit. They got a percentage on serving the Lord." And then he made the application: "Anybody that serves for a commission, for what little bit of glory he can get out of it, he is a merchant and he ought to be cast out of the temple."

I go along with this. If you're serving the Lord, and yet slyly—perhaps scarcely known to you—you're hoping to get just a little five percent commission, then look out! It will chill the power of God in your spirit. You must determine that you will never take any glory, but see that God gets it all.

Now the easiest possible thing is to give a message like this. The hard thing is to make it work in one's own life. Remember that these five vows are not something you write in the back of your Bible and forget. They have to be written in your own blood. They have to be made final, irrevocable. If it only comes off the surface it's no good. Much of our promises come off the *surface. No, no. Let it come out of the depths of your heart, the deep depths of your spirit.*

Theses vows cut against the old human nature. They introduce the cross into your life. And nobody ever walks back from carrying his cross—nobody, ever. When a man takes his cross he's already said goodbye. He's pulled the roll top shut on his desk and said farewell to his wife and children. He's not coming back. The man with the cross never comes back. When you make these vows, remember: They introduce the cross into your life, they strike at the heart of your self-life and there is never a place to go back to. And I say, "Woe to the triflers!"

In America—and maybe in other places, too—so many people are saying, "Try Jesus, try God!" Triflers, experimenters, and tasters they are. Like a rabbit with a half dozen holes so if one is stopped up he can flee to another! No! From the cross, there is no place to flee. You don't "try" Jesus. He's not there to be experimental with. Christ is not on trial. You are. I am. He's not! God raised Him from the dead and forever confirmed His deity and sealed Him and set Him at His own right hand as Lord and Christ. Turn everything over to Him and you'll find your life begin to lift. You'll blossom in a wonderful way.

Now, if you happen to be one of those on whom God has laid His hand for a deeper life, a more powerful life, a fuller life, then I wonder if you would be willing to pray this kind of prayer: "O God, glorify Thyself at my expense. Send me the bill—anything, Lord. I set no price. I will not dicker or bargain. Glorify Thyself. I'll take the consequence."

This kind of praying is simple, but it's deep, wonderful, and powerful. I believe, if you can pray a prayer like that, it will be the ramp from which you can take off into higher heights and bluer skies in the things of the Spirit.[1]

Don't you just love Tozer?

NOTES

Chapter 4   Detour: I Want My Life Back
1. Original story written by author.

Chapter 5   What Now?: Miles to Go before I Sleep
1. Original story written by author.

Chapter 7   Perfect Gifts: Grace Flows Down
1. Original story written by author.
2. Adapted from Matthew 20:1-16.

**Chapter 9   The Great Outdoors: Time Alone
                 . . . with Daddy**
1. Original story written by author.

Chapter 12   Miracles: Boiling an Ocean, Curing World Hunger, and Saving Me
1. Author unknown, "The Price of a Miracle," http://www.snopes.com/glurge/price.htm.

Chapter 13   When the Body Cannot Be Present: Healing Waters
1. Horatio G. Spafford, "When Peace, Like a River" (public domain).

Chapter 16   And Now, Surrender: Perfect Submission, Perfect Delights
1. Original story written by author.

Chapter 17   Living from the Beginning
1. Francie Baltazar-Schwartz, "Attitude Is Everything," http://pr.erau.edu/~madler/attitude.html.

Chapter 18   It's Gonna Be Worth It
1. Eliot Hill, unpublished essay.

An Afterthought
1. A. W. Tozer, "Five Vows for Spiritual Power," http://www.neve-family.com/books/tozer/FiveVows.html.

ABOUT THE AUTHOR

Leslie Haskin achieved great success at Kemper Insurance Company in New York City. She became the Director of Operations and one of the only two African Americans to hold an executive title within the corporation's eastern region.

But 9-11 changed her priorities. In addition to her career, Leslie spends her time in the inner city spreading the message of hope to the homeless and otherwise lost. She is the founder of a ministry designed to provide rehabilitation and healing to women and children who are homeless and victims of domestic violence.

Leslie has appeared at several memorials honoring the victims and survivors of 9-11. She lives in upstate New York.

As someone who was working in the World Trade Center's Tower One on the morning of September 11, 2001, Leslie Haskin will never forget the soul-searing images she witnessed or the horror she endured during her long, panic-driven odyssey toward escape. *Between Heaven and Ground Zero* discloses the harrowing details of Leslie's long journey toward freedom after the plane hit her building.

Suffering from severe Post-Traumatic Stress Disorder, Leslie eventually lost her home, her career, and her life savings. But with faith and medical help, she has emerged from the symptoms of her illness to shine as a remarkable testimony to the enduring legacy of hope. *Between Heaven and Ground Zero* is an unforgettable tale, steeped not in sorrow, but in the overwhelming power of the human spirit to emerge victorious from even the most devastating tragedy.

Between Heaven and Ground Zero
by Leslie Haskin
Bethany House Publishers